# Berlin

Germany

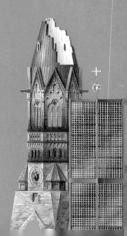

**KNOPF**
CITY GUIDES

**SERIES EDITORS**
EDITORIAL MANAGER:
Seymourina Cruse
BERLIN EDITION:
Caroline Cuny, Mélani Le
Bris, Seymourina Cruse
**GRAPHICS**
Élizabeth Cohat, Yann Le Duc
LAYOUT:
Silvia Pecora
AIRPORT MAPS:
Kristoff Chemineau
MINI-MAPS: Studio Wise
AROUND BERLIN MAPS:
Édigraphie
STREET MAPS:
Touring Club Italiano
Catherine Bourrabier

Translated by Michael Mayor

Edited and typeset by Book
Creation Services, London

Printed in Italy by
Editoriale Libraria

## Authors and editors
**BERLIN**

### Things you need to know:
Roberto Giardina (1)
Since being sent to Germany in 1969 by th
Milan daily *Il Giorno*, Roberto Giardina has
reported on the changing face of Berlin as
correspondent for the *Nazione* (Florence)
and the *Resto del Carlino* (Bologna). A writer
of novels and essays, he has also published a
'guide to loving the Germans'.

### Where to stay and
**After dark:** Ulrike Krause (2)
Born in 1953, Ulrike Krause studied Russian
and politics before teaching at the Hamburg
Institute of Information Technology. As a
freelance journalist, she is a regular
contributor to newspapers and magazines
and has published several tourist guides to
German cities (including Berlin) as well as
some in Eastern Europe.

### Where to eat: Bernd Matthies (3)
Born in Berlin in 1953, Bernd Matthies is
one of Germany's most famous food critics.
Since 1983 he has worked as a reporter on
the Berlin daily *Der Tagesspiegel*.

### What to see: Enno Wiese (4)
Born in 1953, Enno Wiese studied German
and politics before becoming a journalist
and editor. As a freelance journalist, he co-
founded a media agency in Berlin in 1990
along with Ulrike Krause and together they
have written a number of tourist guides.

### Further afield and Where to
shop: Christiane Theiselmann (5)
Christiane Theiselmann lives in Berlin and
specializes in a number of different areas:
travel, nature, figurative art, music and
theater. Today she works in Berlin as a
freelance journalist for several European
magazines and publishers.

# How to use this guide

This guide is divided into eight separate sections: **Things you need to know** (information on travel and living in Berlin); **Where to stay** (hotels); **Where to eat** (restaurants); **After dark** (going out); **What to see** (museums and monuments in the city); **Further afield** (places to visit around Berlin); **Where to shop** (store guide); **Maps** (street maps and plan of the subway).

The **color** of the arrow box matches that of the corresponding dots on the mini-maps.

**In the area** gives you a feel for the location.

### In the area

This was the part of the city in which Christopher Isherwood, author of *Goodbye to Berlin* (the inspiration for Cabaret) lived during the 1930s. Today it is a residential area

The **area** (or the subject on a thematic page) is shown just above the map. A map reference allows you to find places easily in the street map section.

### Augsburgerstraße    F D4

## Where to eat

**Bamberger Reiter** (14)
Regensburger Straße 7, 10777 Berlin
☎ (030) 1842282 ➡ (030) 2142348
Spitzenmöelle **Modern German** ●●●● ⊡ Tue.–Sat. 6–10pm
For more than ten years Franz Bamberger's restaurant has been one of the old eateries in Berlin...

**Europa Center, First Floor** (15)
Budapester Straße 38, 10787 Berlin
☎ (030) 25021020 ➡ (030) 25021166
Ⓜ Kurfürstendamm, Zoologischer Garten **Modern German** ●●●●
⊙ Mon.–Fri. noon–2.30pm, 6–11pm; Sat. noon–2.30pm...

**Speckers Gasthaus** (16)
Kalbacher Straße 15, 10777 Berlin
☎ (030) 2189779 ➡ (030) 2648786
Spitzenmöelle **Modern German** ●●●● ⊡ Tue.–Sat. 7pm–midnight...

**Die Quadriga** (17)
Brandenburger Hof, Eislebener Straße, 10789 Berlin
☎ (030) 2140650 ➡ (030) 21405100
Ⓜ Augsburger Straße **Modern Asian** ●●●● ⊙ Mon.–Fri. 7pm–midnight...

**Not forgetting**
■ **Parkrestaurant** (18) Hotel Steigenberger, Los-Angeles-Platz 1, 10789 Berlin ☎ (030) 2127551 ●●● Light and relaxed hotel menu.

**Not forgetting**
■ **Parkrestaurant**
10789 Berlin ☎ (030) 2...

**Not forgetting** lists places we also recommend, but don't have space to cover in full here.

☎ (030) 25021020 ➡ (030)

Ⓜ Kurfürstendamm, Zoologischer Garten **Modern**
⊙ Mon.–Fri. noon–2.30pm, 6–11pm; Sat. noon–2.3

**Key information** tells you what you need to know about each particular place: the nearest subway station; the price range, accepted means of payment, and the various services and facilities on offer.

The **opening page** of each section gives an index of its contents and some helpful hints.

**Things you need to know** contains information on getting to Berlin and on travel and daily life in the city.

**Thematic pages** pick out a selection of establishments linked by a common element. These are also shown on a simplified map.

Detailed **maps** are given in the eighth section of the guide: a map of the subway and street maps.

## Key

| | |
|---|---|
| ☎ | telephone |
| ➡ | fax |
| ● | price or price range |
| 🕐 | opening hours |
| ☐ | credit cards accepted |
| ☐ | credit cards not accepted |
| V | toll-free number |
| @ | e-mail/website address |

### Access

| | |
|---|---|
| M | subway stations |
| P | parking |
| 🅿 | private parking |
| ♿ | facilities for the disabled |
| ♿ | no facilities for the disabled |
| ➘ | train |
| 🚗 | car |
| ⛴ | boat |
| 🚌 | bus |

### Hotels

| | |
|---|---|
| ☎ | telephone in room |
| ➡ | fax in room on request |
| 🍸 | minibar |
| 📺 | television in room |
| ▥ | air-conditioned rooms |
| 🕐 | 24-hour room service |
| ✖ | caretaker |
| 👶 | babysitting |
| ✚ | meeting room(s) |
| 🐾 | no pets |
| 🍽 | breakfast |
| ☕ | open for tea/coffee |
| 🍴 | restaurant |
| 🎵 | live music |
| ◉ | dance club |
| ✿ | garden, patio or terrace |
| 🏋 | gym, fitness club |
| 🏊 | swimming pool, sauna |

### Restaurants

| | |
|---|---|
| 🥗 | vegetarian food |
| 🌿 | view |
| 👔 | smart dress required |
| 🚬 | smoking area |
| 🍷 | bar |

### Museums and galleries

| | |
|---|---|
| 🏛 | on-site store(s) |
| 🚶 | guided tours |
| ☕ | café |

### Stores

| | |
|---|---|
| 🏬 | branches, outlets |

# Getting there

## Formalities

Visitors to Germany from the EU, the United States, Canada, Australia, and New Zealand will need a passport (valid for at least five years). Visitors from other countries should obtain a visa from their local German consulate. If you are planning to drive in Germany ➡ 13 you will need a valid driver's license and international car insurance.

# 47
# Things
# you need to Know

## Medical care

All EU nationals qualify for free medical treatment on production of an E111 form (available from social security and post offices). Visitors from other countries are advised to take out travel insurance. In an emergency ➡ 15.

## Visitors with disabilities

Berlin's public transport system is well-equipped for visitors with disabilities, and most buses are fitted with safety belts and lifts for people in wheelchairs.

# INDEX A-Z

## Basic facts

Berlin has three airports: Tegel, the largest, situated 5 miles northwest of the city; Tempelhof, situated just 3.5 miles to the south and threatened with closure because of its proximity; and Schönefeld, which formerly served East Berlin and is situated 13.5 miles southeast. Buses and shuttle

# ▶ Getting there

### Tegel
**Enquiries**
☎ Berlin
(030) 41012306
**Lufthansa**
☎ (030) 41010
☎ UK
0345-737747
☎ US
800-645-3880

### British Airways
☎ Berlin
(030) 2540000
☎ UK
0345-789789
☎ US
800-433-7300

### Delta Airlines
☎ Berlin
(030) 2309400
☎ US
800-241-4141
☎ UK
0800-414767

### Lost luggage
☎ (030) 41013113
**Buses**
Nos 109 and X9 to the Zoologischer Garten (U-Bahn/ S-Bahn lines)
30 mins ●
DM3.90

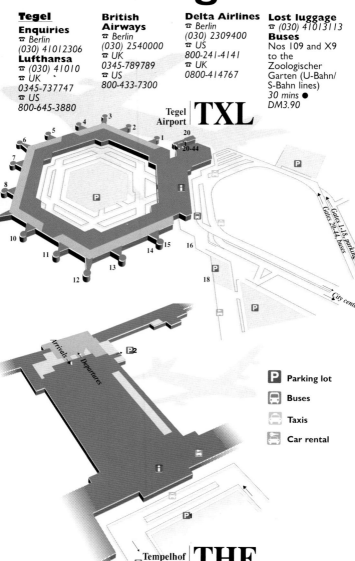

Tegel Airport | **TXL**

Tempelhof Airport | **THF**

**P** Parking lot

▣ Buses

▣ Taxis

▣ Car rental

8

## Traveling to Berlin

services run between the airports, and all three are linked to the city center by bus and subway.

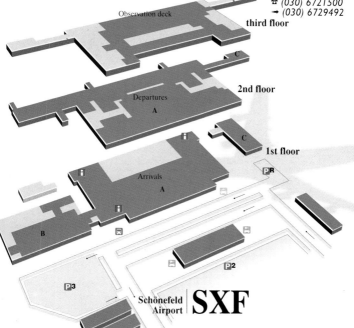

🕐 Daily 5am–11pm, every 10 mins

**Taxis**
At the exit to the terminal building.
● DM25 to Berlin city center (15 mins)

**Car rental**
*Avis*
☎ (030) 60915710
*Hertz*
☎ (030) 60915730
*Sixt*
☎ (030) 60915990

**Post office**
🕐 6.30am–9pm

**Bank**
🕐 8am–10pm

**Hotel**
*Holiday Inn Airport Esplanade*
Rohrdamm 80
13629 Berlin
☎ (030) 383890
➡ (030) 38389900

### Tempelhof
**Enquiries**
☎ (030) 69512288
**Lost luggage**
☎ (030) 69512557
**Subway**
U-Bahn line 6, direct from Adenauerplatz to Kurfürstendamm, Platz der Luftbrücke.
*Less than 15 mins*
**Buses**
At the exit to the terminal building, nos 119, 184, 341 and 104 (night buses N4 and N76) to the center.
*20 mins*
**Taxis**
At the exit to the terminal building.
● DM20 to the center (10 mins)

**Car rental**
*Avis*
☎ (030) 69513814
*Hertz*
☎ (030) 69513818
*Sixt*
☎ (030) 69513471

### Schönefeld
**Enquiries**
☎ (030) 60915112
**Lufthansa**
☎ (030) 60915080
**British Airways**
☎ (030) 2540000
**Delta Airlines**
☎ (030) 2309400
**Lost luggage**
☎ (030) 60916040
☎ (030) 60916038
**Subway**
S-Bahn lines 45 and S9 from Berlin-Schönefeld to Zoologischer Garten 25 mins
● DM8
**Buses**
Nos 160, 163, 602, 735, 736, 737 and 738 to the center.
*45 mins*
Shuttle service to the RB railroad station (Regionalbahn)
**Bank**
🕐 8am–10pm
**Car rental**
*Avis*
☎ (030) 60915710
*Hertz*
☎ (030) 60915730
*Sixt*
☎ (030) 60915990
**Hotel**
*Apart Hotel*
Schwalbenweg 1
12536 Berlin
☎ (030) 6721500
➡ (030) 6729492

Observation deck
**third floor**

C

Departures
A
**2nd floor**

C
**1st floor**

Arrivals
A

B

P3

Schönefeld Airport **SXF**

P2

## Basic facts

The main railroad station in Berlin is the Bahnhof Zoologischer Garten (1), located in the western part of the city. The ICE (2) is the high-speed train run by the Deutsche Bundesbahn (3) (the German national railroad company). Those arriving by car enter the city on the freeway (4), which

# Getting there

## By train

*[Numbers in square brackets refer to the map]*

**Enquiries**
☎ *(030) 27800*

**Reservations**
Train tickets can be booked up to three months in advance.
☎ *(030) 19419*
🕐 *Mon.–Fri. 6am–11pm; Sat. 8am–noon*
@ *www.bahn.de*
● *Reservations for ICE trains DM3 (reservations made separately from ticket purchase DM9)*

## Lost property [4]

*Hackescher Markt S-Bahn subway station*
☎ *(030) 29720621*
🕐 *Mon., Wed.– Thur. 10am–4pm; Tue. 10am–6pm; Fri. 8am–noon*

## Bahnhof Zoologischer Garten [1]

Berlin's main railroad station is on both S-Bahn and U-Bahn lines (subway stations share the name of the railroad station). This is the last stop of the ICE, which travels from

Berlin to Frankfurt in 5 hours and from Berlin to Monaco in just 6 hours 40 minutes.

**Enquiries**
🕐 *5.15am–11pm*
**Left luggage**
● *DM2–DM4 for three days*
**Bank**
🕐 *Mon.–Sat. 8am–9pm; Sun. 10am–6pm*
**Car rental**
🕐 *Mon.–Fri. 8am–6pm; Sat. 8am–noon*
*Avis*
☎ *(030) 2611881*
*Hertz*
☎ *(030) 2611053*
*Sixt*
☎ *(030) 2611357*

## Haupt-bahnhof [2]

Once the main railroad station of East Berlin, it is now the destination for trains coming from southern Europe and the East. There are connections with both S-Bahn and U-Bahn lines.

**Enquiries**
🕐 *5.30am–10pm*
**Bank**
🕐 *Mon.–Fri. 8am–5pm; Sat.–Sun. 8am–1pm*

## Lichten-berg [3]

The railroad station for trains

takes them to the Berliner Ring. ADAC (5), the German Automobile Club, provides a free breakdown service.

to central Europe: Leipzig, Dresden, Prague, Vienna, Budapest, and Omsk (via Russia and Siberia in 92 hours)

**Enquiries**
🕐 5.15am–11pm

## By car

From the Berliner Ring (Berlin's beltway) you can enter the city from a number of directions and join the freeway. Roadworks can create long traffic jams, especially during public and school holidays.

**Freeways**
When Germany was a divided country, freeways were the only legal way of crossing from West to East Berlin.

**A24**
To Hamburg, 180 miles from Berlin. Road in good condition.

**A2**
To Hannover, around 180 miles from Berlin. Road in quite good condition.

**A9**
To Monaco (a little over 300 miles from Berlin) via Leipzig and

Nuremberg. A lot of roadworks.

**A12**
To the Polish border, just 50 miles from Berlin. A word of warning: traffic can be heavy between Berlin and Frankfurt an der Oder.

**A19**
To the north and the beautiful beaches of the Baltic: Stralsund, Warnemunde, and the island of Rügen. Less than 200 miles from Berlin, these towns still bask in a turn-of-

the-century atmosphere.

**Speed limits**
Although there is no legal speed limit on German freeways, German drivers rarely travel faster than 65–80 mph.

**Breakdown services**
☎ (01802) 222222
ADAC (the German Automobile Club) provides a free 24-hour breakdown service. Vehicles that cannot be fixed on the roadside can be towed for a small fee.

## Basic facts

Berlin has a highly efficient public transport system. Below: double-decker buses (1); U-Bahn subway stations (2) for travel underground within Berlin, and S-Bahn stations (3) for travel to the outskirts; the price of tickets (4) varies according to the number of zones (5) crossed;

# Getting around

## Public transport

### Subway U-Bahn

The U-Bahn, opened in 1902, is used by some two million people every day. It has nine lines, readily identifiable by their different colors. The stations are signposted by a white U on a blue background.

### S-Bahn

The S-Bahn, opened in the 1920s, travels to outlying areas. The stations are signposted by a white S on a green background.

### Buses and trams

The city has single-decker, double-decker, and articulated buses. The Express Bus only stops at selected stops. Trams are found only in the former East Berlin, where stops are shown by signs with an H (*Haltestelle*) on them.

### Enquiries

☎ (030)19449

🕒 6am–11pm

### Timetables

The subway runs from 4am to 0.30am. On weekends, the U-Bahn lines 9 and 15 run all night (every 15 mins). Trams and buses run from 4.30am to 0.30am. Those whose number is preceded by N run at night (every 30 mins).

### Tickets

Ordinary tickets for a specified distance or time (two hours) can be bought from newspaper kiosks or ticket machines. Bus tickets can be bought from the driver. Trams have ticket machines on board. For information on passes and other special tickets:

*BVG* Kunden-zentrum Pavillon Berlin Zoo Hardenbergplatz 10787 Berlin

@ info@bvg.de

🕒 8am–10pm

Tickets must be validated by punching them in special machines at the entrance to subway stations and on buses and trams.

### Fares

Children under 6 travel free.

### Zones AB

● *DM2.50 (concessions DM2) to travel 3 subway stations or 6 bus stops; DM3.60 (concessions DM2.40) for a ticket valid for two hours; DM93 for a monthly pass; DM20 for groups of up to five people*

### Zones ABC

● *DM3.90 (concessions DM2.60); DM22.50 for groups of up to five people; DM45 for a weekly pass; DM104 for a monthly pass*

### Welcome Card

*A three-day pass valid on all public transport for one adult and up to three children*

● *DM29*

parking meters
(6) and tickets
(7); taxis (8);
rickshaws (9).

## Lost property

Lorenzweg 5
12099 Berlin-
Tempelhof
☎ (030) 7518021
🕐 Mon.–Tue.,
Thur. 9am–3pm;
Wed. 9am–6pm;
Fri. 9am–2pm

## Taxis

These are easily
spotted by their
signs and cream
color. Taxi ranks
can be found in
front of all the
large hotels. Some
drivers accept
credit cards. If
you're not in a
hurry, try a more
traditional taxi,
the rickshaw!

## Fares

● Pickup charge
DM4; telephone
booking DM2; 1.5
miles or five mins
for DM5; daytime
rate of around
DM1.50–DM2 per
mile; night-time rate
of around
DM1.80–DM2.20
per mile.
Radiotaxi
☎ (030) 210202
☎ (030) 9644
☎ (030) 210101

## Tipping

It is normal to
round the fare up.
For a short
journey in town,
DM2 is enough.

## Cars

It is not advisable
to use your car to
get around the
city center. Traffic
jams are common,
road surfaces are
rough, and parking
is extremely
difficult. It is
illegal to double-
park or to park
on a bend or at
crossroads.
Pedestrians,
particularly in
the former East
Berlin, will not

hesitate to call
the police to have
you fined or
towed away.

## Parking lots

The city has a
number of
underground
parking lots.
Parking meters
are in operation
Mon.–Fri.
9am–7pm, and
Sat. 9am–2pm.
Parking is free on
Sun. and public
holidays.

## Charges

● Parking meters
cost DM2 for 30
mins. Parking lots
cost DM2 for one
hour. Some stores
will refund the cost
of parking for their
customers.

## Traffic regulations

The only surviving
regulation from
the former East
Germany is the
green arrow at

certain traffic
lights that allows
you to turn right
on a red light.
Cycling is popular
and the city is
well provided
with cycle lanes.
If you are driving,
therefore, be
particularly careful
of cyclists, who
expect drivers to
be aware of them.

## Speed limits

In general, 30mph
in the center;
20mph in certain
areas. Traffic fines
are expensive.

## Drinking and driving

It is illegal to
drive with a
blood alcohol
level of more
than 0.8%. Police
checks are very
common,
particularly on
weekends and
public holidays.

# Getting by

## Money

*[The numbers in square brackets refer to the map]*

### Credit cards
All major international credit cards are accepted everywhere, including gas stations.

### Currency
The unit of currency is the Deutschmark (DM) which is divided into 100 Pfennigs. A word of warning: storekeepers do not take kindly to being paid with large denomination notes such as DM500 and DM1000, so try to avoid being given these when changing money.

### Banks
Most banks will change foreign currency. Avoid changing your money in hotels where the rate is not as good.
◷ Mon.–Wed., Fri. 9am–4pm; Thur. 9am–5.30pm

## Bureaux de change
**Zoologischer Garten [5]**
◷ 9am–6pm
*Europa Center* [6]
*Budapester Straße*
◷ 9am–6pm

### Tipping
It is normal to tip at least 5%, commonly by rounding the bill up rather than leaving a tip in the form of change on the table.

## Media

### German press
The main national newspapers are the *Frankfurter Allgemeine* and the *Süddeutsche Zeitung*, and for finance the *Handelsblatt*. For information on entertainment and sports events in Berlin, see the local edition of the *Bild Zeitung*. Berlin's main newspapers are *Der Tagesspiegel*, *Die Welt*, the *Berliner*

*Morgenpost*, the *Berliner Zeitung* and the *Tageszeitung*.

### International press
Foreign daily newspapers can be found on the newsstands around Ku'damm and the Europa Center. The major titles arrive around noon.

### Radio
*Deutsch-landfunk*, a national station, and the local *Deutschlandradio Berlin* broadcast between 5am and 1.05am and 5am and 0.30am respectively. Radio MultiKulti (106.8 Mhz) broadcasts music and news in some 20 languages.

### Television
There are three channels: ARD, ZDF and RTL. Hotels also have a variety of satellite channels such as CNN and its German equivalent N-TV.

## Telephones

### Area codes
To call Berlin from elsewhere in Germany: 030 followed by the number of the person you are calling.
To call Berlin from abroad: dial the international access code followed by 49 (for Germany) and 30 (for Berlin) followed by the number of the person you are calling. To call abroad from Germany: 00 followed by the country code, followed by the area code minus the first 0 (if applicable) followed by the number of the person you are calling.

### National directory enquiries
☎ 01188

### International directory enquiries
☎ 001188

TIERGARTEN

Charlottenburg

7   5

8 6  Kreuzberg

9 10

Wilmersdorf

N

Schöneberg  11 FLUGHAFEN TEMPELHOF

### Collect calls
☎ *010*

### Charges
Calls cost less after 6pm (on a sliding scale) and on holidays. Take care when calling from your hotel room. Calls will cost three or four times more than the normal rate.

### Telephone booths
The old yellow telephone booths are slowly being replaced by the more modern *Telekom* ones that are off-white with a purple stripe. They take both coins and telephone cards (DM10–DM50) which can be bought from post offices and newsstands. Most booths also take credit cards.

### Internet
Some hotels are now connected to the Internet. Internet cafés are popping up all

over Berlin, the most famous still being the first to open:
*Virtuality Café* **[7]**
*Lewishamstraße 1 Berlin (Charlottenburg)*
☎ *(030) 3275143*
⊙ *2pm–1am*

### Post office
Post offices in the main railway stations are open until 10pm. There is no main post office in Berlin.
⊙ *Mon.–Fri. 8am–6pm; Sat. 8am–1pm*

### Late-night shopping
There are no 24-hour stores in Berlin. You can find bread, milk, and other drinks at some gas stations, which stay open at night.

### Tourist information
**Enquiries**
*Berlin-Info* **[8]**
☎ *(030) 250025*

⊙ *Mon.–Sat. 8am–10pm; Sun. 9am–9pm*
*Europa Center* **[6]**
*Budapester Straße*
☎ *(030) 10789*

### Tours of the city
*Severin & Kühn* **[9]**
*Ku'damm 216*
Ⓜ *Uhlandstraße*
☎ *(030) 8831015*
⊙ *Daily from 10am; tours last 3 hours*
● *DM39*

### Boat trips
*Berolina* **[10]**
*Ku'damm 220*
Ⓜ *Kurfürstendamm*
☎ *(030) 8822092*
⊙ *10am–4pm, departures every hour, trips last 90 minutes*
● *DM25*

### Religion
**Protestant Consistory**
*Bachstraße 1–2, 10555 Berlin*
☎ *39 09 13 99*
**Diocese of Berlin**
*Wundtstraße*

*48–50, 14057 Berlin*
☎ *32 00 61 18*
### Jewish community
*Fasanenstraße 79–80, 10623 Berlin*
☎ *88 42 03 32 34*

### Lost property
**Police [11]**
*Platz der Luftbrücke 3*
⊙ *Mon.–Tue. 7.30am–2pm; Wed. noon–6.30pm; Fri 7.30am–noon*

### Emergency services
**Police**
☎ *110*
**Fire**
☎ *112*
**Doctor**
☎ *(030) 19242*
☎ *(030) 310031*
**Pediatrician**
☎ *(030) 610061*
**Dentist**
☎ *(030) 42211437*
**Duty Pharmacy (24 hours)**
☎ *01141*

# Where to stay

## Reservations

The number of rooms available in Berlin has greatly increased over the past few years, but given the number of visitors to the city, you should book your accommodation well in advance. This is particularly true when the city is hosting special events, such as the film festival and Green Week (Grüne Woche), in January and February.

## Hotel restaurants

Hotel restaurants have to cope with extremely demanding foreign travelers. While the food in larger hotels is not always up to scratch, restaurants in mid-sized hotels are often extremely good.

## Prices

The following information is given for each hotel: number of rooms; price range of a double room; number of suites and average price; cost of the least expensive breakfast (often a self-service buffet). All prices include tax.

# Hotels

THE INSIDER'S FAVORITES

## Where to stay in Berlin?

Most hotels in Berlin are found in the Kurfürstendamm area, but you'll have difficulty finding a room for less than DM200 a night. If you are looking for something a little cheaper without being too far out of the center, try the areas of Kreuzberg and Schöneberg (the latter is more lively and will appeal to young visitors). For Bed and Breakfast style accommodation and private apartments, contact: *Mitwohnzentrale, Kurfürstendamm 227-228 ☎ (030) 8826694*

## Youth hostels

Berlin has many good-quality youth hostels situated in the city-center. The only drawback is that they lock their doors early, making it impossible to explore the city's nightlife. Reservations are essential. *Jugendgästenhaus am Zoo, Hardenbergerstraße 9a ☎ (030) 3129410*
For information on other youth hostels, contact:
*Youth Hostel Federation, Tempelhofer Ufer 32, 10963 Berlin ☎ (030) 2649520*

## Basic facts

These hotels combine the facilities of modern establishments with the mystique of decades of tradition. The Schloßhotel Vier Jahreszeiter (in the former West Berlin) has been restored to its former glory. The Hotel Adlon Berlin on the Pariser Platz (in the former East Berlin) has

# Where to stay

### Schloßhotel Vier Jahreszeiten (1)
**Brahmsstraße 10, 14193 Berlin**
**☎ (030) 895840 ➠ (030) 89584800**

🅜 *Grunewald* 🅟 **40 rooms ●●●●● *12 suites* DM950** 📺 *from DM26* ▢ ▣
📞 ▥ 📠 ▥ ⑂ *Vivaldi* ➠ 54 🍽 *Le Tire-Bouchon* 🏊 ✚ ⛷ 🎿 *nearby* ⭐ 🎿

This palatial urban mansion, built at the end of the last century, was transformed into a luxury hotel some 40 years ago. In the 1950s, while it was still called Schloßhotel Gehrhrus, it hosted receptions in honour of national figures such as Theodor Heuss and Konrad Adenauer, and maintained an appropriately stately grandeur for such occasions. Time fades even the grandest establishments, however, and a few years ago the Schloßhotel was renovated at the cost of some 30 million marks (almost $7 million) and reopened at the end of 1992 as the Schloßhotel Vier Jahreszeiten. But this renovation was no mere modernization. The hotel's extraordinary refurbishment was directed by one of the high priests of fashion, Karl Lagerfeld. Every aspect of the hotel's new image was designed by Lagerfeld personally, from the furniture to staff uniforms and letterheads. In recognition of his achievment, the designer was given a suite of rooms to be at his disposal for the rest of his life. This suite is furnished with pieces from his homes in Paris, Monte Carlo, and Brittany. When the great man himself is not in residence, the Karl Lagerfeld suite is available to other guests, but don't despair if this suite is not available on your visit. With their sumptuous beds, priceless wall coverings, and marble bathrooms, all the rooms are equally splendid. Your fellow guests may be equally impressive; the more famous among them have included the King and Queen of Belgium, supermodel Claudia Schiffer, and countless Hollywood stars.

### Hotel Adlon Berlin (2)
**Unter den Linden 77, 10117 Berlin**
**☎ (030) 22610 ➠ (030) 22612222**

🅜 *Unter den Linden* 🅟 **276 rooms ●●●●● *51 suites* DM800** 📺 *DM24–36* ▢
▣ 📞 ▥ ⑂ ⑂ 🍽 ✚ ⛷ 🎿 ▦ 🎿 @ *info@jowi.de/adlon*

The history of the new Hotel Adlon Berlin, situated on the Pariser Platz, goes back even further than that of the Schloßhotel. It is built on the site of the world-famous Grandhotel Adlon, opened in 1907 by Kaiser Wilhelm II. The original hotel remained the most prestigious address in the city until its destruction shortly after World War II. In its heyday, guests rubbed shoulders with millionaires such as the Rockefellers and the Astors, or movie stars such as Charlie Chaplin or the young Marlene Dietrich, who became one of the hotel's more permanent residents. The new Adlon is equally impressive, with its high ceilings, palatial ballroom, and a grand staircase that recalls the glories of the hotel's magnificent past. The walls are covered in golden tapestries and cherry and burr walnut paneling. The two winter gardens in particular – regarded as the hotel's special delight – reflect the romantic legends associated with this extraordinary place. A number of the rooms look out over the famous Brandenburg Gate ➠ 78. Not surprisingly, in such luxurious surroundings, every effort has been made to guarantee a comfortable and profoundly memorable stay in this luxury hotel.

been rebuilt on the site of its famous ancestor. They are two of the finest addresses in the city.

Before the Wall came down, these two hotels were symbols of luxury in the two Berlins: the Schloßhotel in the West and the Adlon in the East.

## In the area

This area in the heart of the city contains a large number of luxury hotels as well as some less expensive places to stay. With many attractions nearby, you'll be spoiled for choice once you step out of the hotel. each day ■ Where to eat ➡ 38 ➡ 44 ■ After dark ➡ 66

# Where to stay

### Hotel Inter-Continental Berlin (3)
**Budapester Straße 2, 10787 Berlin**
**☎ (030) 26020 ➡ (030) 26021159**

🅼 *Zoologischer Garten* 🅿 *444 rooms* ●●●● *67 suites* DM650 🔲 DM32 ▭
▭ ☎ 📶 🍴 *Zum Hugenotten* 🍸 *Marlene Bar* 🔲 ➕ 🏊 🎾 ⚄ ✚ 🚴

This has always been one of the best 'international hotels' in West Berlin. The "Interconti", as it is affectionately known, is used by businessmen as well as tennis champions such as Boris Becker and Steffi Graff, and pop stars such as Michael Jackson. Lovers of good food will appreciate the Hugenotten restaurant and everyone will be impressed by the views from the rooms in the new east wing. Among the Interconti's other attractions is the library, where you can drink tea by the fire in a setting that is more English than German.

### Grand Hotel Esplanade (4)
**Lützowufer 15, 10785 Berlin**
**☎ (030) 254780 ➡ (030) 2651171**

🅼 *Nollendorfplatz* 🅿 *369 rooms* ●●●● *33 suites* DM680 🔲 DM29 ▭ ▭
☎ 📶 🎦 🍴 *Harlekin* ➡ 44 🍸 *Harry's New York Bar* ➕ 🏊 🎾 ✚ 🚴

A luxury hotel with a cosmopolitan atmosphere. Guests who enjoy relaxing over a drink love its watering hole, Harry's New York Bar, owned by the New York establishment of the same name. And for somewhere to eat, there is Berlin's original floating restaurant, the *MS Esplanade*, anchored on the nearby Landwehr canal. Business travelers appreciate the business center that offers up-to-the-minute information on the world's stock markets. And for getting around the city, the hotel can provide the means of transport favored by the king of Tonga and the athlete Carl Lewis: a chauffeur-driven Rolls Royce Silver Wing Mark II at a cost of DM200 an hour.

### Hotel Palace Berlin (5)
**Europa Center, Budapester Straße 38, 10787 Berlin**
**☎ (030) 25020 ➡ (030) 2626577**

🅼 *Kurfürstendamm, Zoologischer Garten* 🅿 *243 rooms* ●●● *42 suites*
DM650 🔲 DM29 ▭ ▭ ☎ 📶 🍴 *First Floor* ➡ 38, *Bon Dia (for breakfast)*
🍸 *Sam's* ➕ 🏊 🎾 *nearby* 🚴

Each of the rooms and suites in this luxury hotel oozes comfort, and your every wish seems to have been taken care of in advance. The pleasures of an opulent breakfast buffet on the terrace are rivaled only by those of having a lighter snack served in bed. The hotel has welcomed many celebrities through its doors, such as the Hollywood star Kevin Costner. It is in the Europa Center, with its tempting stores right at your doorstep.

## Not forgetting

■ **Hotel Berlin (6)** Lützowplatz 17, 10785 Berlin ☎ (030) 26050 ➡ (030) 26052716 ●●● ■ **Sylter Hof (7)** Kurfürstenstraße 114–116, 10787 Berlin ☎ (030) 21200 ➡ (030) 2142826 ●●

# Kurfürstenstraße

**F** C-D4 - **G** C-D1

➡ 72
■ What to
see ➡ 94

Many of Berlin's hotels have their own swimming pool, fitness room, sauna, and massage facilities.

21

## In the area

With its many theaters, movie theaters, boutiques, and department stores, the Kurfürstendamm is one of the busiest areas of West Berlin. Here visitors and Berliners mingle well into the night. ■ Where to eat ➡ 34 ■ After dark ➡ 64 ➡ 68 ➡ 70 ■ What to see ➡ 94

# ► Where to stay

### Kempinski Hotel Bristol Berlin (8)
**Kurfürstendamm 27, 10719 Berlin**
☎ (030) 884340 ➡ (030) 8836075

🅼 *Uhlandstraße* 🅿 *249 rooms* ●●●● *52 suites DM630* 📷 *DM32* 🔲 🖥 ☎
🛗 🍴 *Kempinski Restaurant and Kempinski Eck* 🍸 *Bristol Bar* ♨ ➕ 🏊 ✂ 🎴
★ @ *reservation.ber@kempinski.com*

Hidden behind a modernistic façade dating from the middle of the 20th century is one of Berlin's most famous luxury hotels. The main entrance opens on to the Kurfürstendamm, one of Berlin's most important streets and a vital center of business, culture, and social activity. For more than a hundred years, the Kempinski has been a favorite meeting place for Berlin's residents and visitors alike. Its bar, a popular haunt of VIPs, was completely transformed during renovations in 1993. The elegant bedrooms, all fitted out with marble bathrooms, are furnished in a classic yet modern style.

### Savoy Hotel (9)
**Fasanenstraße 9–10, 10623 Berlin**
☎ (030) 311030 ➡ (030) 31103333

🅼 *Zoologischer Garten 105 rooms* ●●● *20 suites DM520* 📷 *DM28* 🔲 🖥
☎ 🛗 🎰 🍴 🍸 *Times Bar* ➕ 🏊 ✂ ★ 🎿

An elegant hotel with a long tradition of outstanding service, the Savoy was the first hotel in Berlin to boast en suite bathrooms in all its bedrooms. The rooms themselves are spacious and furnished with a meticulous attention to detail. Among the famous guests to stay at the Savoy were the writer Thomas Mann, Herbert von Karajan, and Maria Callas. The hotel has also played a role in Berlin's turbulent history: until 1952, it housed the British army headquarters. The famous Paris Bar ➡ 34 is a stone's throw away.

### Best Western Hotel Boulevard (10)
**Kurfürstendamm 12, 10719 Berlin**
☎ (030) 884250 ➡ (030) 88425450

🅼 *Kurfürstendamm 57 rooms* ●● 🔲 🖥 ☎ 🛗 🍸 ➕

This hotel's two main selling points are its location (not far from the Gedächtniskirche ➡ 94, the Europa Center, and the Kurfürstendamm ➡ 94) and the fact that it is good value for money. Don't bother looking for the reception desk near the entrance; it is on the seventh floor, next to the bar, breakfast room, and covered roof terrace with views over the busy Ku'damm. For those wishing to relax over a drink, the Kranler Café is not far away.

## Not forgetting

■ **Hotel am Zoo (11)** Kurfürstendamm 25, 10719 Berlin ☎ (030) 884370 ➡ (030) 88437714 ●●●
■ **Hotel Concept (12)** Grolmanstraße 41–43, 10623 Berlin ☎ (030) 884260 ➡ (030) 88426500/820 ●●●

Elegant interiors and inviting little nooks hide behind the façades and buildings at the far end of the Ku'damm.

## In the area

The Kurfürstendamm is only one face of the cosmopolitan city of Berlin.
It would be a mistake to ignore the little streets running off it,
particularly Meinekestraße. Here you will find not only hotels and
boutiques, but also some fine restaurants.

# ▶ Where to stay

### Mondial (13)

**Kurfürstendamm 47, 10707 Berlin**
☎ (030) 884110 ▪ (030) 88411150

M *Uhlandstraße* P **74 rooms** ●● *1 suite DM700* ▢ ▢ ☎ ▯ ▥
▯ *Kräutergarten* ▯ *Terrassen-Boulevard-Café* ✚ ≋

This relaxing hotel has a swimming pool, sunbeds, and a thalassotherapy
center where you can enjoy an invigorating massage. The rooms and
bathrooms are all of a good size and can accommodate people with
physical disabilities. For those who enjoy a night at the theater, the
Theater am Kurfürstendamm and the Komödie ▪ 66 are directly
opposite the hotel.

### Bleibtreu Hotel (14)

**Bleibtreustraße 31, 10707 Berlin**
☎ (030) 884740 ▪ (030) 88474444

M *Uhlandstraße* **51 rooms** ●●● *9 suites DM454* ▨ *DM25* ▢ ▢ ☎ ▥ ▯
▯ *Restaurant 31* ▪ 36 ▯ *Blue Bar* ≋ ▦

Opened in 1955, this hotel decided on a modern look, importing
beautifully designed furniture from Italy. At the end of a tiring day,
residents can choose between the Turkish baths and the anti-stress
therapies offered in a spotless health club. A florist and small
delicatessen are also at your
disposal. The Bleibtreustraße
itself is one of the prettiest

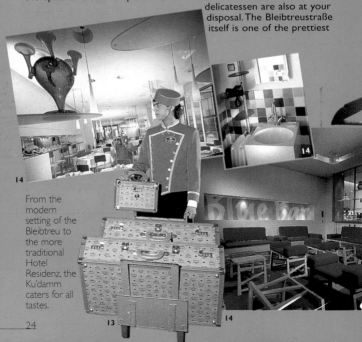

From the
modern
setting of the
Bleibtreu to
the more
traditional
Hotel
Residenz, the
Ku'damm
caters for all
tastes.

- Where to eat ➡ 36
- After dark ➡ 66 ➡ 68
- What to see ➡ 94
- Where to shop ➡ 122

streets crossing the Ku'damm ➡ 94: with its small stores, inviting restaurants and *Kneipen* (bistros) it is the perfect setting for a leisurely evening stroll.

## Hotel Residenz Berlin (15)
### Meinekestraße 9, 10719 Berlin
☎ (030) 884430 ➡ (030) 8824726

Ⓜ *Kurfürstendamm* 🅿 **79 rooms** ●● **9 suites** *DM450* 🌑 *DM22* ▭
▢ ☎ 📠 🍴 *Restaurant Grand Cru* 🍸 *Residenz Bar* @ *info@hotel-residenz.com*

Of the streets around Kurfürstendamm ➡ 94, the Meinekestraße is one not to be missed. Among its architectural attractions is the beautiful *belle époque* building that now houses the Hotel Residenz Berlin. The hotel is a particular favorite of people working in the media. The atmosphere is both intimate and cosmopolitan, the service faultless, and the rooms spacious. Around the hotel there are many restaurants, but the finest is the hotel's own, the Grand Cru, furnished in *Jugendstil* fashion and known by gourmets the world over.

## Not forgetting

- **Berlin Mark Hotel (16)** Meinekestraße 18–19, 10719 Berlin ☎ (030) 880020 ➡ (030) 88002804 ●●
- **Hotel Meineke (17)** Meinekestraße 10, 10719 Berlin ☎ (030) 882811 ➡ (030) 8825716 ●●

## In the area

While the atmosphere around the Ku'damm, Tauentzienstraße, and Wittenbergplatz is like that of any large international city, the nearby district of Schöneberg captures the true essence of Berlin. It is home to a number of fine restaurants and stores, and the area is one of the

# Where to stay

### Steigenberger (18)
**Los-Angeles-Platz 1, 10789 Berlin**
☎ (030) 21270 ➡ (030) 2127117

Ⓜ *Augsburger Straße* Ⓟ **386 rooms** ●●● *11 suites* DM750 🔾 DM29 ▭ ▣ ▢ 🔂 🏨 *Parkrestaurant* ➡ 38 🍴 ✚ ♒

This hotel, situated between the Ku'damm ➡ 94 and the KaDeWe ➡ 120, is one of the most highly rated in the area. It is centrally located yet on a quiet square, and combines elegant decor with the quality of service you would expect in a top-class hotel. Tina Turner and Luciano Pavarotti have stayed here while on concert tours. The visitors' book also bears witness to a visit by Marlon Brando.

### Sorat Art'otel Berlin (19)
**Joachimstaler Straße 29, 10719 Berlin**
☎ (030) 884470 ➡ (030) 88447700

Ⓜ *Kurfürstendamm* Ⓟ **133 rooms** ●● ▭ ▣ ▢ 🔂 Ⅲ 🏨 *Anteo* 🍴 ✚
@ *Headoffice@SORAT-Hotels.com*

Housed in a converted dairy, this hotel is decorated in an unabashed modern style. The rooms are furnished with bold and creative furniture, and the walls are adorned with original works of art by the Berlin artist Wolf Vostell.

### Brandenburger Hof (20)
**Eislebener Straße 14, 10789 Berlin**
☎ (030) 214050 ➡ (030) 21405100

Ⓜ *Augsburger Straße* Ⓟ **86 rooms** ●●● ▭ ▣ ▢ 🔂 🏨 *Die Quadriga* ➡ 38 🍴 *Piano Bar* ✚ ✖

This small hotel recently opened in a former palace built during the reign of Kaiser Wilhelm, not far from the Ku'damm ➡ 94. The moment you see the entrance, flanked by columns, you will be struck by the sheer beauty of the building. The classical splendor of the exterior is in stark contrast to the simplicity of the Bauhaus-inspired decoration of the bedrooms. The Wintergarten, with a Japanese garden in one corner, is the setting for musical evenings, art exhibitions, and antique fairs.

### Alsterhof Ringhotel Berlin (21)
**Augsburger Straße 5, 10789 Berlin**
☎ (030) 212420 ➡ (030) 2183949

Ⓜ *Augsburger Straße* Ⓟ **200 rooms** ●●●● ▭ ▣ ▢ 🔂 🏨 *Alsterstuben* 🍴 *Scala* ✚ ♒ ⛷ @ *www.top-hotels.de/alsterhof*

A good hotel and an ideal place to stay for shoppers (the KaDeWe ➡ 120 is less than a ten-minute walk away) and night owls (many restaurants and *Kneipen* are also nearby).

## Not forgetting

■ **Hotel Ambassador Berlin (22)** Bayreuther Straße 42–43, 10787 Berlin ☎ (030) 219020 ➡ (030) 21902380 ●●

liveliest in the capital.
- Where to eat ➡ 38
- Where to shop ➡ 120

It is not unusual to find beautiful swimming pools in Berlin hotels, like this one in the Steigenberger; the Alsterhof also has one.

The area between Friedrichstraße and the Gendarmenmarkt is in the process of being redeveloped: large hotels, shopping malls, and major department stores are already sprouting up. A number of restaurants have also opened. ■ Where to eat ➡ 48 ■ After dark ➡ 60 ➡ 61

# Where to stay

### Grand Hotel Berlin (23)
**Friedrichstraße 158–164, 10117 Berlin**
☎ (030) 20270 ➡ (030) 20273419

Ⓜ *Friedrichstraße* Ⓟ **358 rooms** ●●● **35 suites** *DM900* 🅦 *DM29* ▫ ▪ ☎
▪ ▥ 🍴 *Coelln; Die Goldene Gans Forellenquintett* Ⓨ ▫ *Café Bauer* ✚ ≋
✕ ✱

An impressive stairway leads up from the entrance hall to take you to the rooms that are all furnished in a different style: rococo in one, *belle époque* in another, art nouveau in a third. But the showpiece of the hotel remains the Shinkel suite, in which all the furniture is inspired by the work of the famous Berlin architect of that name. Appreciating the hotel's imposing name, former guests have included Leonard Bernstein and Jane Fonda. The hotel's fleet of Mercedes is placed at guests' disposal.

### Berlin Hilton (24)
**Mohrenstraße 30, 10117 Berlin**
☎ (030) 20230 ➡ (030) 20234269

Ⓜ *Stadtmitte* Ⓟ **460 rooms** ●●●● **42 suites** *DM600* 🅦 *DM32* ▫ ▪ ☎
▪ ▥ 🍴 *Mark Brandenburg; Ristorante Fellini; La Coupole* ➡ 48 Ⓨ *Kaminbar*
✚ ≋ ✕ ⊘ ≋

Although this hotel only opened its doors a few years ago, it has managed to successfully re-create the famous charm of the great luxury hotels of Old Berlin. Located not far from one of the most attractive squares in the city (the Gendarmenmarkt ➡ 80), its facilities for guests include access to its winter gardens which have their own waterfall. More mundane services include offices that business travelers can rent by the day.

### Four Seasons Hotel (25)
**Charlottenstraße 49, 10117 Berlin**
☎ (030) 20338 ➡ (030) 20336166

Ⓜ *Französische Straße* Ⓟ *162 rooms* ●●●● *42 suites* *DM800*
🅦 *DM25–DM31 à la carte* ▫ Ⓞ ▪ ☎ ▥ ▪ ▥ 🍴 *Seasons* ➡ 48
Ⓨ ✚ ≋ ✕ ✱ ≋ @ *www.fshr.com*

This hotel, designed in a supremely grand style that is perfectly in keeping with the other important buildings in this neighborhood, has a façade made of stone chosen to match that of the French and German churches ➡ 80 and even the Schauspielhaus. The interior is dominated by gray and pink marble, softened by precious rugs and richly upholstered furniture. The lobby is decorated with antiques, 19th-century paintings, and Dresden china figurines. Once inside the bedrooms, marble decoration predominates again, and is especially imposing in the bathrooms

## Not forgetting
■ **Maritim Proarte Hotel Berlin (26)** Friedrichstraße 151, 10117
Berlin ☎ (030) 20335 ➡ (030) 20334209 ●●

➡ 62 ➡ 72 ■ What to see
➡ 80 ■ Where to shop
➡ 128 ➡ 130 ➡ 131

M *Friedrichstraße*
29  M *Friedrichstraße*
Georgenstraße
Hegel-
platz
Dorotheenstraße
26
11
30
Universitätsstr.
44
31  8  43
Unter  4  den Linden
3
5  5  STAATS-
OPER
23
25
Behrenstraße
41  39
23  25  Markgrafenstr.  Straße
Französische  Straße
*Französische* M
*Straße*  22  42
Jägerstr.
27  26  6
Taubenstraße  *Hausvogteiplatz* M
24  Hausvogtei-
platz
*Stadtmitte* M  Mohrenstraße  N
43  24  ↑

23

23

The elegant
staircase of the
Grand Hotel
and the piano
bar of the
Berlin Hilton.

23

24

25

BERLIN HILTON

24

25

25

## In the area

This area was once the heart of working-class East Berlin, but today only a few traces of the pre-war Alexanderplatz remain. Amid the socialist architecture there are many romantic corners to explore, and, toward Oranienstraße, there are many *Kneipen* (small restaurants) in which to

# ▶ Where to stay

## Hotel Luisenhof (27)
### Köpenicker Straße 92, 10179 Berlin
### ☎ (030) 2415906 ⇒ (030) 2792983

Ⓜ *Märkisches Museum* Ⓟ **26 rooms** ●● ▢ ▣ ☎ ⬆ �� *Alexanderkeller* Ⓨ *Wintergarten* ✚

Built in 1822, the Luisenhof is one of the oldest buildings in the Luisenstadt. The beauty of this newly renovated hotel is surpassed only by the warmth of the welcome it offers and the continuing friendliness of its staff. Guests are invited to start the day in the appropriate manner with a satisfying breakfast served in the winter garden, and they have an opportunity (which should not be missed) to finish it with a drink in the vaulted room of the Alexanderkeller.

## Mercure Alexander Plaza Berlin (28)
### Rosenstraße 1, 10178 Berlin
### ☎ (030) 2415067 ⇒ (030) 2423804

Ⓜ *Hackescher Markt* Ⓟ **74 rooms** ● *18 suites and 5 apartments* DM355 Ⓥ DM22 ▢ ▣ ☎ ⅲ ⬆ ⶲ Ⓨ ✚ ⚌ ⚌

This fine hotel opened its doors to the public during the summer of 1997, after a refurbishment that successfully transformed a former furriers' premises into one of the most convenient and practical hotels in the city. The Rosenstraße, on which it is situated, is one of the oldest streets in Berlin, not far from the Alexanderplatz and Unter den Linden ⇒ 80. The hotel caters for business travelers, and everything has been done to ensure that it is possible to mix business with pleasure while staying here. Each room is equipped with a large desk, and the hotel offers both secretarial services and short-term office rental. The hotel's five rentable apartments all have kitchenettes, which will appeal to longer-term guests.

## Forum Hotel Berlin (29)
### Alexanderplatz 8, 10178 Berlin
### ☎ (030) 23890 ⇒ (030) 23894305

Ⓜ *Alexanderplatz* Ⓟ **1006 rooms** ●●● *12 suites* DM300 ▢ ▣ ☎ ⬆ ⶲ *Humboldt's, Zille-Stube* Ⓨ Ⓞ *Disco Chip* ⚌ ⚌ ⊞ ⚌

The Forum Hotel is one of the largest hotels in Berlin both in capacity and height – the only construction taller than this skyscraper is the nearby television tower. The hotel's attractions include a casino on the 38th floor and the 'Chip Disco' offering a wonderful panoramic view over Berlin, which is ablaze with lights at night. It is also well located for other sights worth visiting in the area: the Nikolaiviertel ⇒ 84, Unter den Linden ⇒ 80, and Museum Island ⇒ 82.

## Not forgetting

■ **Hotel Berliner Congress Center (30)** Märkisches Ufer 54, 10179 Berlin ☎ (030) 27580 ⇒ (030) 27582170 ●●
■ **Art'otel Ermeler Haus Berlin (31)** Wallstraße 70–73, 10179 Berlin ☎ (030) 240620 ⇒ (030) 24062222 ●

soak up the local atmosphere.
■ What to see ➡ 82 ➡ 84

27

28

29

27

Contrasting styles of architecture in the former East Berlin.

27

27

29

**Credit cards**
Restaurants accept all major credit cards. Credit cards can also be used to withdraw money from one of the many ATMs ➤ 14 in the city center.

# ➡ Where to eat

**Tipping**
It is usual to round up the bill, adding a tip of 10%.

**Currywurst**
The quintessential Berlin meal is a tasty sausage, cut into slices, served with a tomato sauce and sprinkled with curry powder. You can find it at any hour of the day or night at one of the many *Imbiß*, or stands, on the streets of the city. A melting pot of nations and cultures, Berlin is also famous for its kebabs.

## 'Genießen auf gut deutsch'

Try some good old German cooking! Berlin's chefs delight in serving up *aal grün* (eels in a herb sauce) or one of their other specialties prepared with fish from local lakes and rivers. Some restaurants serve an *altberliner* buffet: bread spread with melted fat, potato and apple pancakes, meatballs with mustard, marinated herring and pickles.

# 66

# Restaurants

## THE INSIDER'S FAVORITES

# INDEX BY TYPE

In the heart of the busy Schöneberg district lie two havens of tranquility;
the Savignyplatz and Kanstraße, one of the streets that crosses the
square. They are the ideal locations for a quick lunch break or an evening
meal, in one of the many restaurants and cafés that have opened there.

# Where to eat

## Paris Bar (1)
### Kantstraße 152, 10623 Berlin ☎ (030) 3138052 ➡ (030) 3132816

🅼 *Zoologischer Garten* **French** ●●● 🕓 *Daily noon–1am*

For decades, the Paris Bar has been the most famous restaurant in
Berlin, as much for its simple cooking (onion soup, oysters, steak…) as
for its bistro atmosphere. It is expensive and reservations are essential.

## Fischküche (2)
### Uhlandstraße 181–183, 10623 Berlin
### ☎ (030) 8824862 ➡ (030) 8860429

🅼 *Uhlandstraße* **Traditional German and French** ●●● 🕓 *Mon.–Sat.
noon–3pm, 6–11.30pm*

In a building made entirely of steel and glass located at the back of the
Kempinski hotel ➡ 22, the Fischküche serves a selection of light and
simple fresh fish dishes: shrimp salad, *Steinbutt* (giant turbot) in a
champagne and mustard sauce, and sole meunière. Good wines are
available by the carafe.

## Carpe diem (3)
### Savigny-Passage 576–577, 10623 Berlin
### ☎ (030) 3132728 ➡ (030) 3132628

🅼 *Savignyplatz* **Mediterranean** ●● 🕓 *Tue.–Sat. noon–1am*

Under the arches of the restored railroad station, you can sit at solid
wood tables and chose from a creative selection of tapas and fish dishes
from the south of France, as well as from a more traditional, if
somewhat adapted, menu (basquaise chicken, paella). To drink, there is
a large selection of champagne and schnapps.

## Tai Ji (4)
### Uhlandstraße 194, 10623 Berlin ☎ (030) 3132881 ➡ (030) 3132856

🅼 *Uhlandstraße* **Chinese** ●● 🕓 *Tue.–Sun. noon–11pm* 🍴

Tucked away in a semicircular glass building, the Tai Ji's menu is for the
more adventurous. You can sample dishes with unusual names such as
'Eight drunks immortalized on a hot plate,' served with mushrooms,
bamboo shoots, or lightly steamed soybeans. The house specialty is *knack-
reis*, or fried rice with vegetable sauce.

## Not forgetting

■ **Florian (5)** Grolmanstraße 52, 10623 Berlin ☎ (030) 3139184 ●●
*A favorite haunt of artists. Southern German home cooking.*
■ **Risto-Vinoteca Cristallo (6)** Knesebeckstraße 3, 10623 Berlin
☎ (030) 3126117 ●● *Modern Italian cooking. Large selection of wines.*
■ **Ottenthal (7)** Kantstraße 153, 10623 Berlin ☎ (030) 3133162 ●●
*Regional dishes from Austria.*
■ **Good Friends (8)** Uhlandstraße 181–183, 10623 Berlin
☎ (030) 88551510 ●●● *Cantonese specialties served on the second floor of the
Franco-German restaurant, the Fischküche (see above).*

■ Where to stay ➤ 22
■ After dark ➤ 64 ➤ 66
➤ 72 ➤ 74 ■ Where to
shop ➤ 124 ➤ 126 ➤ 130

Enjoy fresh fish dishes in the pleasant surroundings of the Fischküche.

FISCHKÜCHE

Fasanenstraße is the most fashionable street in Berlin, as notable for its galleries as it is for its eateries. Many of its restaurants continue the cultural theme of the street, offering interesting lecture programs as well as delicious food. ■ Where to stay ➡ 24 ■ After dark ➡ 64 ➡ 66

 # Where to eat

### Kulturrestaurant Goethe (9)
**Fasanenstraße 73, 10719 Berlin**
**☎ (030) 88550067 ➠ (030) 88683543**

Ⓜ *Uhlandstraße* **Italian** ●●● 🕒 *Daily noon–midnight*

The name of this restaurant recalls Goethe's love of Italy. The owners aim to combine cooking with culture, regularly hosting talks, musical evenings, and exhibitions. The chef, Renzo Pasolini, offers light, modern Italian dishes with a French influence, such as sturgeon served in a foie gras sauce. Good wines and quick service.

### Diekmann (10)
**Meinekestraße 7, 10719 Berlin ☎ (030) 8833321 ➠ (030) 85729477**

Ⓜ *Kurfürstendamm* **Traditional German** ●● 🕒 *Mon–Sat. noon–11.30pm*

Opened in a store that once sold colonial artifacts, the Diekmann has successfully integrated the original decor, displaying old advertising signs on its walls. The atmosphere is intimate and cozy. Favorite dishes include game pâté, *Tafelspitz* with potato stock, or saddle of rabbit in thyme. The wine list is varied.

### Aida (11)
**Ludwigkirchstraße 6, 10719 Berlin**
**☎ (030) 8850616 ➠ (030) 8834971**

Ⓜ *Spichernstraße* **Arabic and Mediterranean** ●● 🕒 *Daily 5pm–1am* 🗙

At Aida, East meets West in tastefully furnished surroundings. Traditional Arabic dishes from *Kicherebsencreme* (hummus) to stuffed dates and lamb are served alongside more original recipes (Haloumi cheese grilled with eggplant, scampi, and couscous).

### Café im Literaturhaus (12)
**Fasanenstraße 23, 10719 Berlin**
**☎ (030) 8825414 ➠ (030) 8818882 (Literaturhaus)**

Ⓜ *Kurfürstendamm* **Modern German** ●● 🕒 *Daily 9.30am–midnight* 🗙

The Literaturhaus is one of Berlin's major cultural institutions. It combines a library, reading rooms, a delightful café with a garden, and a fine restaurant in a building dating from the end of the 19th century. The restaurant offers a light, delicate menu, including dishes such as monkfish served on a bed of asparagus risotto, and leg of rabbit served with mushrooms. The wine list is excellent. In the summer, the terrace is the perfect place for an enjoyable meal.

### Not forgetting

■ **Restaurant 31 (13)** Bleibtreustraße 31, 10707 Berlin
☎ (030) 88474603 ●● *Creative organic food served in the restaurant of the Bleibtreu Hotel* ➡ 24.

## Ku'damm (Adenauerplatz)    **F** C1 - D2

■ Where
to shop
➡ 122
➡ 124

The fitting sign for Enoiteca Il Calice, an Italian restaurant with a wonderful cellar.

41

## In the area

In the 1920s, Charlottenburg was nicknamed Charlottengrad because of the large White Russian population who had settled there after the Revolution. Today it is an elegant residential area where you can find some excellent traditional restaurants.

# Where to eat

### Bruno (24)
**Sophie-Charlotten-Straße 101, 14059 Berlin**
☎ (030) 3257110 ➠ (030) 3226895

Ⓜ *Westend* **Modern Italian** ●●●● 🕐 *Tue.–Fri. 6pm–midnight*

Bruno Pellegrini's place is without a doubt the best Italian restaurant in town. The menu is based on the freshest seasonal produce. Bass is served with Tuscan beans and truffles, pasta is made from chestnut flour as in Liguria, and you can even try onions simmered in chocolate. The wine list, full of comments and observations, makes for good reading and for even better tasting!

### Hitit (25)
**Knobelsdorffstraße 35, 14059 Berlin**
☎ (030) 3224557 ➠ (030) 3211846

Ⓜ *Sophie-Charlotte-Platz* **Turkish** ●● 🕐 *Daily noon–1am* 🅧

With the exception of kebab stalls, Turkish restaurants are hard to find in Berlin, despite the fact that some 200,000 Turks now live in the city. The Hitit, not far from the Charlottenburg Schloss ➠ 96, offers a fine menu served in interesting surroundings (paintings inspired by Hittite reliefs, a waterfall running down a marble wall). Recommended dishes include the sliced liver and the veal with vegetables.

### Ponte Vecchio (26)
**Spielhagenstraße 3, 10585 Berlin ☎ (030) 3421999**

Ⓜ *Bismarckstraße* **Italian** ●●●● 🕐 *Mon., Wed.–Sun. 6.30–11pm*

Enter this light wood building and discover a corner of Tuscany in Berlin. The owner, Walter Mazza, is always at hand to advise and sing the praises of his native cuisine. Make sure you try the seafood cocktail, the grilled guinea fowl, or the veal kidneys cooked in garlic and parsley.

### Trio (27)
**Klausenerplatz 14, 14059 Berlin ☎ (030) 3217782**

Ⓜ *Westend* **Modern German** ●●● 🕐 *Mon.–Tue., Fri.–Sun. 7pm–1am*

This small but elegant restaurant has already established its culinary reputation. Siegfried Stier has created a varied menu that owes its influences to France and southern Germany (goose liver braised with apples, fillet of fish in a Riesling sauce, free-range chicken served with salad). The wine list is excellent.

## Not forgetting

■ **Don Camillo (28)** Schloßstraße 7–8, 14059 Berlin ☎ (030) 3223572 ●●● *Don Camillo serves good traditional Italian food. The restaurant is particularly inviting in summer when meals are served outside under the arbor.*
■ **Le Piaf (29)** Schloßstraße 60, 14059 Berlin ☎ (030) 3422040 ●● *A typical French bistro. Good simple food and a friendly atmosphere.*

# Charlottenburg

E A-B4 - F A1 - C2

■ After dark ➡ 61
■ What to see
➡ 96 ➡ 97

**24** Reproductions of ancient Hittite relief carvings decorate the walls of Hitit, the most famous Turkish restaurant in Berlin.

## In the area

The Tiergarten ➡ 90, situated in the heart of Berlin at the foot of the Wall, is one of the most beautiful parks in Europe. Enjoy fresh air and lush greenery as you try out a few typical German restaurants? ■ Where to stay ➡ 20 ■ After dark ➡ 66 ➡ 70 ➡ 72

# Where to eat

### Am Karlsbad (30)
**Am Karlsbad 11, 10785 Berlin** ☎ **(030) 2645349** ➡ **(030) 2644240**

Ⓜ *Kurfürstenstraße* **Modern German** ●●● 🕓 *Mon.–Fri. noon–3pm, 6–11.30pm; Sat. 6pm–1am*

This semicircular glass building, tucked away in a courtyard, is home to the best restaurant between the Kulturforum ➡ 92 and the massive building sites of the Potsdamer Platz ➡ 88. The menu includes a carefully chosen selection of international dishes along with some German and Austrian recipes, such as saddle of veal on a bed of asparagus and *Steinbutt* (turbot) in red wine. A word of advice: save room for the excellent desserts! There is also a good wine list.

### Café Einstein (31)
**Kurfürstenstraße 58, 10785 Berlin**
☎ **(030) 2615096** ➡ **(030) 2619176**

Ⓜ *Nollendorfplatz* **Austrian** ●● 🕓 *Daily 10am–2am*

Housed in a *Jugendstil* (art nouveau) building in the heart of a lively area this Austrian café is on a par with those in Vienna. The menu includes Austrian café specialties along with some simply presented modern dishes (monkfish with eggplant, *Wiener Schnitzel*). In summer, meals are served outside in the charming garden. This popular restaurant is often crowded, and the service can be a little slow.

### Harlekin (32)
**Grand Hotel Esplanade, Lützowufer 15, 10785 Berlin**
☎ **(030) 25478858** ➡ **(030) 2651171**

Ⓜ *Nollendorfplatz* **Modern international** ●●●● 🕓 *Tue.–Fri. 6–11pm* 🍸 *Tue.–Sat. noon–4am* ➡ 20

The quality of food and service in some of Berlin's hotel restaurants rank them among the best places to eat in the city. The large, colorful Harlekin is a good example. The chef, Kurt Jäger, has come up with a subtle and creative mixture of dishes: soup served with fresh goat's cheese, turbot in pesto, breast of pigeon served with calves' sweetbreads. As the evening draws on, the party atmosphere in the neighboring Harry's New York Bar becomes contagious.

### Merz am Ufer (33)
**Schöneberger Ufer 65, 10785 Berlin**
☎ **(030) 2613882** ➡ **(030) 7514231**

Ⓜ *Kurfürstenstraße* **Southern German** ●● 🕓 *Tue.–Fri. noon–1am; Sat.–Sun. 6pm–1am*

This discreet restaurant offers good quality cooking based mainly on southern German recipes, but with the odd hint of Italy here and there. Take your pick from saddle of veal with mushrooms, osso bucco served with steamed green vegetables, or risotto. In summer, ask to sit outside on the terrace overlooking the Landwehrkanal and take in the view of the new Nationalgalerie ➡ 92.

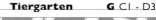

■ What to see
➡ 92 ➡ 93

31

A lively Harlequin is the inspiration behind the colorful restaurant to which he lends his name.

## In the area

Kreuzberg is one of the friendliest, liveliest areas of Berlin. For years it has been home to radicals, students, and artists, as well as a large Turkish community. Today it is attracting the attention of property developers.
■ After dark ➡ 70 ➡ 72

 # Where to eat

### Altes Zollhaus (34)
**Carl-Herz-Ufer 30, 10961 Berlin**
**☎ (030) 6923300 ➠ (030) 6923566**

Ⓜ *Prinzenstraße* **Modern German** ●●●● 🕓 *Tue.–Fri. 6pm–1am*

The Altes Zollhaus is located in the historical heart of the city in a former customs house, now a protected building. With a menu inspired by recipes from the province of Brandenburg, it has justifiably earned its place among the best restaurants in Berlin. Herbert Beltle has come up with some subtle and well-conceived specialties that make this establishment well worth a visit: consider warm smoked salmon on a bed of lettuce, whiting cooked in truffle butter, or Brandenburg crispy duck. There is a large selection of good wines and the service is quick and efficient.

### Austria (35)
**Bergmannstraße 30, 10961 Berlin ☎ (030) 6944440**

Ⓜ *Gneisenaustraße* **Austrian** ●● 🕓 *Daily 7pm–1am*

A warm welcome and a simple rustic setting, with a dining room decorated with wood paneling and cuckoo clocks, give this establishment an Austrian feel that matches its name. This is also reflected in the authentic style of the cooking, developed in keeping with the spirit of Austrian cuisine.

### Tres Kilos (36)
**Marheinekeplatz 3, 10961 Berlin**
**☎ (030) 6936044 ➠ (030) 6936045**

Ⓜ *Gneisenaustraße* **Tex-Mex** ●● 🕓 *Daily 6pm–2am* ✗

Tex-Mex has been popular in Berlin since the beginning of the 1990s, and this restaurant was one of the vanguard which established the style. Sit among the cacti, listening to lively Mexican music, as you sample the flavorful and fiery cuisine. Later, cool your taste buds with refreshing margaritas or simply enjoy your tequila straight.

### Osteria No. 1 (37)
**Kreuzbergstraße 71, 10965 Berlin ☎ (030) 7869162**

Ⓜ *Platz der Luftbrücke* **Italian** ●● 🕓 *Daily noon–2am*

In days gone by, the artists who lived in the Kreuzberg district would meet up around the tables of the Osteria No.1 for a drink and a pizza. Today its diners prefer something a little more original and distinctive, such as carpaccio with pomegranate, ox tongue in green sauce, rabbit with walnuts and polenta. In summer, you can dine outside in the attractive courtyard.

## Not forgetting

■ **Riehmer's (38)** Hagelberger Straße 9, 10965 Berlin ☎ (030) 7868608
●● *Inexpensive German food.*

Osteria № 1
Piero Da Villa
Pablo Angulo
Kreuzbergstr. 71
1000 Berlin
Telefon (030) 786 91 62
Telefax (030) 786 61 84

37

37

35

34

Long ago, the Gendarmenmarkt ➥ 80 was considered one of the most beautiful squares in Europe. Today it is in the center of a dynamic neighborhood, determined to become the heart of the new Berlin.
■ Where to stay ➥ 28 ■ After dark ➥ 60 ➥ 62 ➥ 72

# Where to eat

### Borchardt (39)
**Französische Straße 47, 10117 Berlin**
☎ (030) 20397117 ➥ (030) 20397150

[M] *Französische Straße* **French and German** ●●● 🕐 *Daily 11.30am–1am*

The dining room, supported by four imposing columns, was once frequented by the Huguenot community. Today it plays host to an illustrious clientele. The menu offers a wide range of international specialties, with strong Asian and vegetarian influences.

### Königin Luise (40)
**Opernpalais, Unter den Linden 5, 10117 Berlin**
☎ (030) 20268443 ➥ (030) 2044438

[M] *Hausvogteiplatz* **German** ●●● 🕐 *Tue.–Fri. 6pm–midnight*

Tucked away in the magnificent historical setting of the Opernpalais are several cafés and restaurants. Of these, the Königin Luise is worth a visit, if only to admire its splendid interior. However, the traditional German menu (loin of beef in fennel, veal in herbs) doesn't always live up to its surroundings.

### Seasons (41)
**Four Seasons Hotel, Charlottenstraße 49, 10117 Berlin**
☎ (030) 20336363 ➥ (030) 20336166

[M] *Französische Straße* **Modern international** ●●● 🕐 *Daily 11.30am–2.30pm, 6–11.30pm* [X]

This restaurant was an immediate success when it opened in 1996 in the new Four Seasons Hotel ➥ 60. Try some of its excellent regional specialties (pike cooked in potatoes) and vegetarian creations (napoleon of green vegetables in pesto). There is a good wine list.

### Vau (42)
**Jägerstraße 53-54, 10117 Berlin**
☎ (030) 2029730 ➥ (030) 20297311

[M] *Stadtmitte* **Modern German** ●●●● 🕐 *Mon.–Sat. noon–3pm, 7pm–1am*

The Vau opened its doors to the public in 1997 in the Bürgerhaus am Gendarmenmarkt ➥ 80 and is currently trying to catch up with the front runners. The Hamburg chef, Anton Viehauser, combines regional German cooking with modern international dishes. The lunchtime menu at DM20 is very good value.

## Not forgetting

■ **La Coupole (43)** Berlin Hilton, Mohrenstraße 30, 10117 Berlin ☎ (030) 20234647 ●●●● *Modern cooking, views over the Gendarmenmarkt.*
■ **Einstein Unter den Linden (44)** Unter den Linden 42, 10117 Berlin ☎ (030) 204363235 ●● *A well-situated café-restaurant.*

What to see ➡ 80

Where to shop
➡ 128 ➡ 130 ➡ 131

Restaurant
KÖNIGIN LUISE

40

39

39

42

41

42

Since 1989, the
Gendarmenmarkt,
home of
the Vau, has
once again
become the heart
of Berlin.

## In the area

The Mitte district, full of historic monuments, was almost totally deserted when the city was divided into two. Since reunification, it has been given a new lease of life and has again become a hive of activity.

■ Where to stay ➡ 30 ■ After dark ➡ 62 ➡ 64 ➡ 66 ➡ 68 ➡ 70

 # Where to eat

### Hackescher Hof (45)
**Rosenthaler Straße 40-41, 10178 Berlin**
**☎ (030) 2835293 ➡ (030) 2835294**

Ⓜ *Hackescher Markt* **Traditional German** ●● *Daily 5pm–2am*

This restaurant offers a brasserie-style setting and a menu to cater for all tastes, from breakfast to a three-course dinner, and in the evening, a special menu to whet the appetite of any gourmet. Good German wines.

### Modellhut (46)
**Alte Schönhauser Straße 28, 10119 Berlin ☎ ➡ (030) 2835511**

Ⓜ *Weinmeisterstraße* **International and modern Italian** ●●
◯ *Daily 7pm–midnight*

The gilt decor of this bistro-restaurant, in a former hat factory, re-creates the style of the 1930s. The creative menu is both Italian (risotto with greens and mushrooms, lamb with polenta) and international (salmon in saffron and orange).

### Oren (47)
**Oranienburger Straße 28, 10178 Berlin**
**☎ (030) 2828228 ➡ (030) 28599313**

Ⓜ *Oranienburger Straße* **North African** ●● ◯ *Daily 10–1am*

The Oren is a veritable institution in this cosmopolitan district. It offers a wide range of vegetarian dishes as well as a number of specialties from North Africa and the Middle East (such as eggplant stuffed with a mushroom sauce), all washed down with wines from the Golan Heights and beer from Israel.

### Kamala (48)
**Oranienburger Straße 69, 10117 Berlin**
**☎ (030) 2810704 ➡ (030) 44342090**

Ⓜ *Oranienburger Straße* **Thai** ● ◯ *Daily 11.30am–midnight*

Tucked away behind the Synagogue ➡ 86, this restaurant (a cellar with a bar and kitchen) is easy to miss – which is a pity since it serves some of the best Thai food in the city. Try the chicken stew served in a pineapple, or beef in oyster sauce. There is a wide choice of drinks.

## Not forgetting

■ **Beth Café (49)** Tucholskystraße 40, 10117 Berlin ☎ (030) 2813135
● *Traditional kosher Jewish cooking.*
■ **Skales (50)** Rosenthaler Straße 13, 1011 Berlin ☎ (030) 2833006 ●●
*Unpretentious, friendly atmosphere and good Greek food.*
■ **Café Aedes (51)** Hackesche Höfe, Rosenthaler Straße 40–41, 10178
Berlin ☎ (030) 2822103 ● *A popular meeting place, always crowded.*

➡72 ➡74
■ What to
see ➡82
➡86

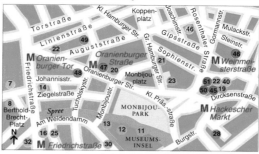

45

48

45

48

46

47

51

## In the area

With a population of artists and intellectuals, Prenzlauer Berg buzzes with activity. It is not surprising that the first mumblings of political discontent in the former East Berlin were heard here.
■ After dark ➡ 70 ➡ 72

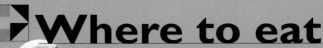

# Where to eat

53

53

A Far Eastern atmosphere whets the appetite for the exotic dishes of the Maothai.

55

55

### Je länger je lieber (52)
**Göhrener Straße 1, 10437 Berlin ☎ ➡ (030) 4412295**

Ⓜ *Eberswalder Straße* **Modern German** ●● Ⓢ *Daily 6pm–midnight*

The decor and the food combine to make this restaurant well worth a visit. The fact that it is not really on the tourist trail is an added bonus. The menu includes both traditional dishes (beef bourguignon, breast of lamb stuffed with fruit) and something for a more adventurous palate (pike with vegetables and pasta, sweet pepper and basil soup). Wines are served by the carafe.

### Maothai (53)
**Wörther Straße 30, 10405 Berlin**
**☎ (030) 4419261 ➡ (030) 44342090**

Ⓜ *Senefelderplatz* **Thai** ●●● Ⓢ *Mon.–Fri. noon–11.30pm; closed third Sun. of every month* ✗

Thai cooking that doesn't pull any punches: the strongest spices are handled with the greatest care. Specialties include a spicy soup made with shrimps, coriander, and lemon, to be followed by curried chicken in coconut or steamed pike with celery and ginger.

### Rosenbaum (54)
**Oderberger Straße 61, 10435 Berlin**
**☎ (030) 4484610 ➡ (030) 4493077**

Ⓜ *Eberswalder Straße* **Modern German** ●●● Ⓢ *Mon.–Sat. 6pm–midnight*

One of the best restaurants in the eastern part of Berlin with a menu that draws inspiration from French, southern German, and Italian cooking: consider confit of duck served with seasonal vegetables, or sea bream cooked in butter, tomato, and tarragon. Excellent deserts, all as light as a feather!

## **Ostwind** (55)
### Husemannstraße 13, 10435 Berlin ☎ (030) 4415951

**M** Eberswalder Straße **Chinese** ●● 🕑 Mon.–Sat. 6pm–1am; Sun. 10am–1am
**Ⅹ**

The Ostwind is the only one of the restaurants well worth visiting in the late 19th-century buildings along the Husenmannstraße. Tucked away in a basement, it serves authentic Chinese food, unmodified for Western tastes. Highly recommended dishes include noodles with lotus roots, Tong-Ku mushrooms and Gan Bien beef with soybeans and ginger. If you are in a hurry, try the Ostwind bistro.

## Not forgetting

■ **Pasternak (56)** Knaackstraße 22–24, 10405 Berlin ☎ (030) 4413399 ● Simple Russian bistro-style cooking.
■ **Offenbach-Stuben (57)** Stubbenkammerstraße 8, 10437 Berlin ☎ (030) 4458502 ●● Filling German food.

The most beautiful areas of parkland in Berlin are found in Grunewald and Zehlendorf. They are also prestigious residential areas, home to famous artists and politicians. Here luxury restaurants and bars rub shoulders with traditional *Kneipen*.

# Where to eat

## Cristallo (58)
**Teltower Damm 52, 14167 Berlin**
☎ (030) 8156609 ➡ (030) 8153299

M *Zehlendorf* **Italian** ●●● 🕒 *Daily noon–midnight*

This conventionally elegant restaurant was the first to introduce Berliners to modern Italian cooking. But recently, the chef has put aside experimentation in favor of a more traditional menu: white truffle and ricotta ravioli, monkfish with ratatouille, beef en croûte with mushrooms and bacon. The wine list is as good as ever, with a wide selection of wines from northern Italy.

## Grand Slam (59)
**Gottfried-von-Cramm-Weg 47–55, 14193 Berlin (Wilmersdorf)**
☎ (030) 8253810 ➡ (030) 8266300

M *Grunewald* **Modern international** ●●●●● 🕒 *Tue.–Sat. 6.30pm–midnight*

The decor of an English manor provides the setting for this elegant restaurant. The chef, Johannes King, is one of the finest in Berlin. His specialties include fish and scallops in lemongrass, saddle of venison with onions, and rabbit with mushrooms. In the summer, reserve a table on the terrace overlooking the Hubertussee.

## Remise Glienicke (60)
**Königstraße 36, 14163 Berlin** ☎ (030) 8054000 ➡ (030) 8059901

M *Wannsee* **International and German** ●●● 🕒 *Wed.–Sun. noon–9pm*

Thanks to Franz Raneburger (owner of the Bamberger Reiter ➡ 38), this restaurant, situated in the grounds of the Schloss Klein Glienicke, has made a successful comeback in recent years. Regional Austrian cooking can be eaten on the large terrace with views over the grounds of the Schloss.

## Vivaldi (61)
**Schloßhotel Vier Jahreszeiten, Brahmsstraße 10,**
**14193 Berlin** ☎ (030) 89584520 ➡ (030) 89584800

M *Grunewald* **Modern international** ●●●●● 🕒 *Daily 6.30pm–midnight*

The Schloßhotel Vier Jahreszeiten ➡ 18, with its magnificent decor created by, Karl Lagerfeld, one of the great gurus of twentieth-century fashion design, is unquestionably the finest hotel in Berlin. Its restaurant, the Vivaldi, shares the same stylish decor although it must be said that the cuisines does not always live up to the hotel's superlative reputation. The chef, Georg Fuchs, favors a conventional menu and prepares traditional Austrian dishes, such as turbot with spaghetti squash, or beef with goose livers. There is a good wine list.

## Not forgetting
■ **Halali (62)** Königstraße 24, 14163 Berlin ☎ (030) 8053125 ●●
*Good Austrian home cooking.*

In this part of Berlin, you can choose between rustic eateries or more formal, elegant restaurants.

## Basic facts

Before World War II, Wedding, in the far north of Berlin, was a bastion of the working class movement. Since 1989, the area has been rediscovered by Berliners. Reinickendorf, north of Wedding, is dotted with fields, meadows, and forests, and includes some elegant residential areas.

# ➤ Where to eat

### Enoteca Reale (63)
**Gottschedstraße 2, 13357 Berlin**
☎ (030) 4617433 ➡ (030) 4652366

Ⓜ *Nauener Platz* **Modern Italian** ●●●● Ⓞ *Mon.–Sat. 7pm–1am*

From the outside, this restaurant looks a bit like a seedy night club, but don't be put off – ring the bell – because this place is worth a visit. Its designer decor is rather cold but the quality of the food, inspired by recipes from the Veneto and Tuscany (scallops, perch with shrimp in *prosecco* sauce) is perfectly complemented by superb wines. The service is good and the menu priced accordingly.

### Piazza Italiana (64)
**Oranienburger Chaussee 2, 13465 Berlin-Glienicke**
☎ (030) 4044613 ➡ (030) 4044614

Ⓜ *Hermsdorf* **Italian** ●● Ⓞ *Daily 9am–midnight*

Until 1989, Berlin was cut off from outlying districts by the Wall and its watchtowers. It is on this 'border' that you can today find one of the best restaurants in the city. Piazza Italiana, open from breakfast until late at night, is a cross between a trattoria, a pizzeria, a delicatessen, and a wine bar. The pizzas, still cooked over a wood fire, are amazing. But don't overlook the appetizers, pasta, and meat and fish dishes. They hold some pleasant surprises!

## Rockendorf (65)
**Düsterhauptstraße 1, 13469
Berlin
☎ (030) 4023099
➠ (030) 4022742**

Ⓜ *Waidmannslust* **International
and Modern German** ●●●●●
🕐 *Tue.–Sat. noon–2pm,
7–11.30pm*

Despite growing competition
and some financial problems,
Siegfried Rockendorf has
remained a name to be
reckoned with in the world of Berlin restaurants for more than a
decade. His parfait of goose liver, lobster in champagne and cognac,
saddle of venison in pepper, and ricotta mousse are all wonderful. They
are served in an elegant if somewhat fussy setting. To complement such
fine food there is an excellent selection of wines.

## Landhaus am Poloplatz (66)
**Am Poloplatz 9, 13465 Berlin ☎ (030) 4019035 ➠ (030) 4019036**

Ⓜ *Frohnau* **Italian** ●●● 🕐 *Tue.–Fri. 4–11pm; Sat.–Sun. noon–11pm*

The Landhaus offers all the charm of a traditional Italian menu: *vitello
tonnato* (slices of veal in a tuna sauce), *saltimbocca* (paupiette of veal),
along with some more original dishes (carrot and *prosecco* soup,
medallions of veal in ginger and lemon sauce). The service is wonderfully
efficient. The location and surroundings of the Landhaus are also
delightful and, for those wishing to spend longer in this beautiful setting,
the Landhaus also has a number of comfortable bedrooms.

# After dark

## See you at the Kneipe

The Kneipe is to Germany what the pub is to Ireland: *the* place to meet friends. Berlin is home to thousands of *Kneipen*, all full of Berliners enjoying a drink and chatting well into the night. There is nowhere better to catch up on what's happening in Berlin.

## Variety

Musicals, lavish productions, variety shows, operas, concerts… Berlin nightlife has something for everyone. Check the main local daily newspapers ➡ 14 for entertainment listings. The largest ticket agency is: *Europa Center, Budapester Straße* ☎ *(030) 10789*

**One hour before the performance starts...**

...box offices open to sell the last remaining tickets for that day's performance but you'll need to get there early to stand any chance of getting a ticket. To avoid disappointment, reserve seats a few days in advance by simply calling the theater or the Berlin Ticket agency: ☎ (030) 23088230.

# 49
# Nights out
## THE INSIDER'S FAVORITES

## Program of cultural events

| | | | |
|---|---|---|---|
| **February** | Internationale Filmfestspiele (International Film Festival) | **May** | Theatertreffen (Theater Festival) |
| | | **June** | Pfingsfrühkonzerte (Whitsun concerts) |
| **April** | Berliner Kunsttage Freie Berliner Kunstaussellung (various art exhibitions) | **September** | Berliner Festwochen (operas, ballets, concerts, plays) |
| | | **November** | Jazz-Fest Berlin (Jazz Festival) |

t was during the reign of Frederick the Great (1740–86) that Berlin saw
the dawning of a new musical age. Philosopher, musician and Francophile,
the king clearly favored culture over rules and regulations, in sharp
contrast to his father, the 'soldier king'. Today, Berlin is home to three

# After dark

## Philharmonie (1)
### Matthäikirchstraße 1, 10785 Berlin ☎ (030) 254880/25488132

🅜 *Potsdamer Platz* 🚌 *142, 148, 248* 🕐 *Box office 3.30–6pm, Sat.–Sun. 11am–2pm* ● *prices vary* 🍸

The Philharmonie, a masterpiece of acoustic technology, opened in 1963 and is one of the largest concert halls in the world. Thanks to the talent of Herbert von Karajan (1907–89), the Berlin Philharmonic Orchestra has been one of the finest in the world since the 1970s. The present conductor is Claudio Abbado. The Kammermusiksaal, adjoining, is reserved for chamber music.

## Konzerthaus am Gendarmenmarkt (2)
### Gendarmenmarkt 2, 10117 Berlin
### ☎ (030) 2030921-01/02

🅜 *Hausvogteiplatz, Stadtmitte* 🕐 *Box office noon–8pm; Sun. noon–4pm and 1 hour before the performance* ● *prices vary* 🍸

Designed in 1818–21 by Schinkel and rebuilt after World War II. the Konzerthaus reopened its doors to the public in 1984. It now hosts concerts, a variety of cultural events, and fashion shows. It is also home to the Berliner Singakademie.

## Staatsoper Unter den Linden (3)
### Unter den Linden 7, 10117 Berlin
### ☎ (030) 20354555

🅜 *Friedrichstraße* 🕐 *Box office 10am–6pm Sat.–Sun. 2pm–6pm) and 1 hour before the performance* **Reservations** *10am–8pm; Sun. 2pm–8pm* ● *prices vary*

This, the first public opera house in Prussia, was founded in 1742 by Frederick II. The musical director, Daniel Barenboim, presents big names and new talent. The program includes operas, concerts, and ballet.

## Concerts and operas

world-famous opera companies
and several large orchestras
and continues to delight in its
musical legacy.

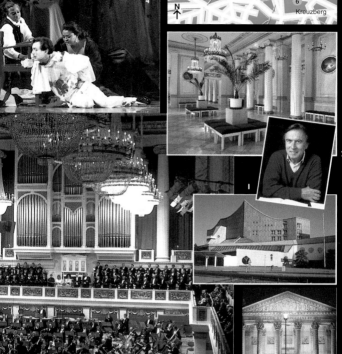

## Deutsche Oper (4)
### Bismarckstraße 35, 10627 Berlin ☎ (030) 3410249

Ⓜ *Deutsche Oper* 🕐 *Box office 11am and 1 hour before the performance; Sun. 10am–2pm* ● *prices vary* 🍽

The building of the Wall deprived West Berlin of a major opera
company until this new company rose from the ashes of the former
Charlottenburg opera, opening in this venue in 1961. You can hear
operas by Mozart, Verdi, Wagner, under the baton of some of the world's
best conductors. Great acoustics.

## Not forgetting

■ **Komische Oper (5)** Behrenstraße 55–57, 10117 Berlin
☎ (030) 47021000/0180-5304168 *Until 1975, this was the sounding board for
Walter Felsenstein, the reformer of post-war theater in East Germany. Classical
operas, original operettas and ballets.* ■ **Tanztheater Hebbel-Theater
(6)** Stresemannstraße 29, 10963 Berlin ☎ (030) 25900427 *One of the best
venues for dance and pop and rock concerts.*

## Basic facts

Following World War II, the division of the city led to a rich dramatic output, with each half striving to assert its cultural autonomy. Although Berlin theater went into decline following reunification, it is once again becoming the scene of dramatic innovation.

# After dark

### Deutsches Theater/Kammerspiele (7)
**Schumannstraße 13, 10117 Berlin ☎ (030) 28441225**

Ⓜ *Friedrichstraße* 🕐 **Box office** *noon–6pm; Sun. 3pm–6pm and 1 hour before the performance* ● *prices vary* Ⓨ

The oldest theater in Berlin (1883) became world-famous during the 1920s when it was run by Max Reinhardt. In the 1970s and 1980s, the likes of Heiner Müller and Frank Castorf left their mark, and today, the present director, Thomas Langhoff, gives classical plays from Germany and around the world a modern interpretation.

### Berliner Ensemble (8)
**Bertolt-Brecht-Platz 1, 10117 Berlin ☎ (030) 2823160**

Ⓜ *Friedrichstraße* 🕐 **Box office** *11am–6pm; Sun. 3pm–6pm and 1 hour before the performance* ● *prices vary* Ⓨ

The Berliner Ensemble was founded in 1949 by Bertolt Brecht and his wife, the actress Helene Weigel, and became famous for its productions of Brecht's plays. However, since reunification, and the death of Heiner Müller in 1995, the constant changes in management have caused more excitement than any of its recent productions.

### Volksbühne (9)
**Rosa-Luxemburg-Platz, 10178 Berlin ☎ (030) 2476772, 24065661**

Ⓜ *Rosa-Luxemburg-Platz* 🕐 **Box office** *noon–6pm, evenings* ● *prices vary* Ⓨ

Originally hailed as the 'people's theater' and made famous by Erwin Piscator, its first director and creator of 'epic theater'. The Volksbühne is one of the most avant-garde stages in Berlin thanks to the original productions by the present director, Frank Castorf.

### Schaubühne am Lehniner Platz (10)
**Kurfürstendamm 153, 10709 Berlin ☎ (030) 890023**

Ⓜ *Adenauerplatz* 🕐 **Box office** *11am–6.30pm; Sun. 3pm–6.30pm, evenings* ● *prices vary* Ⓨ

Under the direction of Peter Stein, this was the Mecca of classical German theater during the 1970s. Today, that status seems to be a thing of the past, even though Luc Bondy's production of *Sculßchor*, a play by Botho Strauss, was well received by audiences. The hopes of finding renewed success now lie with the present director, Andrea Brecht.

## Not forgetting

■ **Maxim-Gorki-Theater (11)** Am Festungsgraben 2, 10117 Berlin ☎ (030) 20221115 *Russian realist texts.*

■ **Schloßparktheater (12)** Schloßstraße 48, 10165 Berlin ☎ (030) 7931515 *Director: Heribert Sasse. From modern plays to Shakespeare. Out-of-the-ordinary productions.*

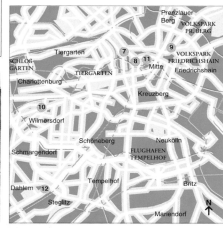

The theatrical genius
of social and political
pioneers, such as
Piscator and Brecht,
still influences the
Berlin stage.

## Basic facts

In the 1920s, Berlin was considered the European capital of entertainment, a place where pleasure and audacity went hand in hand. Today it would appear that the German capital has once again become a cultural magnet, attracting shows from all over Germany and the United States.

# After dark

### Theater des Westens (13)
**Kantstraße 12, 10623 Berlin ☎ (030) 8822888**

Ⓜ *Zoologischer Garten* 🕐 **Box office** *Tue.–Sat. noon–6pm; Sun. 2–4pm; evenings* **Reservations** *10am–6pm; Sat. 10am–4pm* ● *prices vary* 📶

Opened in 1896, this was originally the home of comedies and operettas. It has since become one of the most prestigious venues for musicals in Berlin thanks to shows such as *Cabaret* (1987) and *La Cage aux Folles*. This stage features German productions, Broadway and West End musicals, and classical operettas.

### Friedrichstadtpalast (14)
**Friedrichstraße 107, 10117 Berlin**
**☎ (030) 232620 / 23262474 ➡ (030) 2823997**

Ⓜ *Oranienburger Tor, Friedrichstraße* 🕐 **Box office** *Mon. 1pm–6pm; Tue.–Fri. 1pm–7pm; Sat.–Sun. 2pm–7pm; evenings* **Reservations** *Mon.–Sat. 10am–6pm* ● *prices vary* 📶

Once the most popular venue for light entertainment in East Germany, today this is the home of the world's largest dance troupe, whose glitzy reviews make use of all the latest special effects, expensive sets, and world-famous artists.

### Schiller Theater Musical (15)
**Bismarckstraße 110, 10625 Berlin**
**☎ (030) 31113111 / 31907049**

Ⓜ *Ernst-Reuter-Platz* 🕐 **Reservations** *from 10am* ● *prices vary* 📶

The Schiller Theater, once famous for its highbrow productions, is now one of the best venues for musicals in town. Famous touring troupes bring successes such as *West Side Story*, *42nd Street*, and *Fame* over from the United States.

### Metropol-Theater (16)
**Friedrichstraße 101, 10117 Berlin ☎ (030) 20246117**

Ⓜ *Friedrichstraße* 🕐 **Box office** *Tue.–Sat. 11am–7pm; Sun. and public holidays 3–5.30pm, and 1 hour before the performance* **Reservations** *Tue.–Sat. 11am–6.30pm* ● *prices vary* 📶

With musicals like *My Fair Lady* and operettas such as *Der Vogelhändler*, the Metropol (today under the direction of the opera singer, Renée Kollo) continues in the popular tradition that established the theater's success at the end of the 19th century.

## Not forgetting

■ **Musical-Theater Berlin (17)** Schaperstraße 24, 10719 Berlin ☎ (030) 8842080 Shakespeare & Rock 'n' Roll *will probably run for many years to come.*

■ **Musical Space Dream (18)** Flughafen Tempelhof, Columbiadamm 2–6, 10965 Berlin ☎ (0180) 5221313 Space Dream: *as of February 1997, high-tech special effects in an airport hangar.*

Tiergarten

Mitte

14

16

TIERGARTEN

Charlottenburg

15    13

Kreuzberg

17

Wilmersdorf

18

Schöneberg

FLUGHAFEN
TEMPELHOF

N

13

13

14

14

14

# After dark

### Renaissancetheater (19)
**Hardenbergstraße 6, 10623 Berlin ☎ (030) 3124202**

**M** *Ernst-Reuter-Platz* ○ **Box office** *evenings* **Reservations** *10.30am–7pm; Sat. 10am–7pm; Sun. 5–7pm* ● *prices vary* **Y**

The new artistic director has issued his mission statement: to present contemporary plays that are both entertaining and thought-provoking. Recent productions have included everything from classic pieces to new plays by German and European writers.

### Komödie and Theater am Kurfürstendamm (20)
**Kurfürstendamm 206, 10719 Berlin ☎ (030) 47021010**

**M** *Uhlandstraße* ○ **Box office** *10am–7pm; Sun. 3–7pm, evenings* **Reservations** *9am–8pm; Sun. 3–8pm* ● *prices vary* **Y**

The Komödie and the Theater am Kurfürstendamm are the main venues for light comedies in Berlin. Here, German TV stars tread the boards alongside some of the big names of the German stage. Musicals and revues re-create the atmosphere of Berlin in the 19th century.

### Wintergarten (21)
**Potsdamer Straße 96, 10785 Berlin ☎ (030) 23088230**

**M** *Kurfürstenstraße* **Reservations** *Berlin Ticket ☎ (030) 23088230* ● *prices vary* **Y**

The director Peter Schwenkow has called upon the talents of the director of the Roncalli circus to help produce a top-quality variety show in the tradition of pre-war Berlin. Also appearing on the bill are acrobats, magicians and stand-up comedians.

### Chamäleon Varieté (22)
**Rosenthaler Straße 40-41, 10178 Berlin ☎ (030) 2827118**

**M** *Weinmeisterstraße, Hackescher Markt* ○ **Box office** *Mon.–Thur. noon–9pm; Fri.–Sat. noon–midnight; Sun. 4–9pm* ● *prices vary* **Y**

The newest of Berlin's many variety clubs presents a mixed program. Located in a slightly dusty 1920s ballroom in the Hackeschen Höfen, the list of performers includes magicians, acrobats, and stand-up comedians.

## Not forgetting

■ **Bar Jeder Vernuft (23)** Schaperstraße 24, 10719 Berlin ☎ (030) 8831582 *Songs and comedy performed under a 100-year-old glass ceiling to audiences sitting on threadbare velour.*
■ **Kabarett Die Stachelschweine (24)** Europa Center, Budapester Straße 38, 10787 Berlin ☎ (030) 2614795 *Wolfgang Gruner and his famous Stachelschweine (porcupine), popular cabaret in the west during the 1970s.*
■ **Kabarett Die Distel (25)** Friedrichstraße 101, 10117 Berlin ☎ (030) 2044704 *Typical East-German style cabaret shows.*

21

21

21

19

21

22

19

22

19

19

## Basic facts

Berliners have always loved the movies, and the city can boast several elegant, old cinemas, particularly around the Kurfürstendamm, that have recently been renovated. A multiplex is also being built on the Potsdamer Platz that will house several screens and theaters.

# After dark

## Zoopalast (26)
### Hardenbergstraße 29a, 10623 Berlin ☎ (030) 25414777

Ⓜ️ *Zoologischer Garten* 🕐 *times vary* ● *prices vary*

The Zoopalast is one of the most famous movie theaters in the city. A popular haunt of Berliners during the Weimar Republic, it hosted the premiere of *Blue Angel* in the presence of an up-and-coming young actress, Marlene Dietrich; before the film finished, Dietrich left to take a train to Bremen and from there headed off to the United States where she stayed until the end of the war, despite repeated 'invitations' from the Nazis who wanted to see her back on German soil. The Zoopalast, with its large screen, excellent acoustics, and superb laser show, is still the first choice for Berlin's premieres. It will host the Berlinale (an international film festival) until the year 2000, when this prestigious event is scheduled to move to the new complex in the Potsdamer Platz.

## Titania Palast (27)
### Schloßstraße 4–5, 12163 Berlin ☎ (030) 79090666

Ⓜ️ *Walter-Schreiber-Platz* 🕐 *times vary* ● *prices vary*

German and international film stars flocked here after World War II when the Berlinale was held here. The cinema was renovated at the beginning of the 1990s and is today one of the finest movie theaters in town. What better way to end a day's shopping in the Schloßstraße, one of the main shopping streets in Berlin, than by resting your feet and taking in a movie?

## Waldbühne (28)
### Am Glockenturm, 14053 Berlin ☎ (030) 810750

Ⓜ️ *Olympiastadion* 🚌 *149* 🕐 *times vary* **Reservations** *Berlin Ticket* ☎ *(030) 23088230* ● *prices vary*

Movies are projected onto a huge screen in this amphitheater in the middle of the countryside. An extraordinary venue, it seats 20,000 and as well as acting as an open-air movie theater, it hosts many music events. Concerts by some of the biggest names in pop music, from the Rolling Stones to Sting and Tina Turner. Large classical concerts are also held here, attracting many well-known names, both in the audience and among the performers.

## Not forgetting

■ **Astor (29)** Kurfürstendamm 217, 10719 Berlin ☎ (030) 8811108 *A beautiful movie theater in the middle of the famous Berlin avenue. Recently renovated. Quality movies.*
■ **Gloria Palast (30)** Kurfürstendamm 12, 10719 Berlin ☎ (030) 8854319 *Two large and comfortable auditoriums showing a good selection of movies.*

SCHLOß
GARTEN
OLYMPIA-
STADION
Charlottenburg
TIERGARTEN
**28**
**26**
**30** **29**
GRUNEWALD
Wilmersdorf
Schöneberg
Schmargendorf
**27**
N

ZOO PALAST

IMPERIUM
SCHLÄGT ZURÜCK

DAS PREMIERENKINO

**26**

**26**

The 1930s amphitheater of
Waldbühne hosts both rock
concerts and recitals of
classical music.

**28**

TITANIA PALAST

**27**

**27**

**27**

## Basic facts

It is often said that pop, rock, and jazz are as much a part of Berlin as the famous *currywurst*. Before 1989, this was particularly true in West Berlin, while the authorities in the East did all they could to quash any musical innovation. The popularity of the autumn jazz festival, which

# After dark

### Quasimodo (31)
**Kantstraße 12a, 10623 Berlin ☎ (030) 3128086**

**M** *Zoologischer Garten* **○** *Café 5pm–1am* **Music club** *from 9pm, closed Sun. and Mon. for concerts* **⊡**

Fans of jazz and blues will find something to suit all tastes in the quiet, friendly, intimate atmosphere of this very traditional club. It prides itself on having welcomed some big names from the worlds of jazz, rock and blues. Regulars recall the legendary jazz session improvised by Prince in 1988 and the memorable performances by Chet Baker and Dizzy Gillespie.

### Tränenpalast (32)
**Reichstagufer 17, 10117 Berlin ☎ (030) 2386211**

**M** *Friedrichstraße* **○** *times vary* **⊡**

This glass building owes its name (the palace of tears) to the harrowing farewells that took place during the years when the Wall existed. It was in this hall that visitors from the West said goodbye to their friends in the East before passing through passport control at the border posts on Friedrichstraße. Nowadays the building hosts concerts, exhibitions, and techno parties.

### Franz Club (33)
**Schönhauser Allee 36–39, 10435 ☎ (030) 4428203**

**M** *Eberswalder Straße* **○** *Tue.–Sat. from 10pm* **Ⓨ ⊡**

Situated in the premises of the former Schultheiss brewery, the Franz Club stages a different concert every night. Jazz, blues and rock are performed by both amateur and professional musicians. It draws a sizable proportion of its audience from among the residents of Prenzlauer Berg, the Greenwich Village of Berlin. If you want to unwind without shouting yourself hoarse, there is always the club's quieter *Kneipe*.

### Junction Bar (34)
**Gneisenaustraße 18, 10961 Berlin ☎ (030) 6946602**

**M** *Gneisenaustraße* **○** *from 8pm* **⊞ ⊡**

The Junction Bar stages a live concert every night. At the beginning of the week, the focus is on jazz, followed from Thursday to Saturday by other types of music. On Sunday, the week ends with a disco. For those looking for a snack, try the delicious nachos.

## Not forgetting

■ **Metropol/Loft (35)** Nollendorfplatz 5, 10777 Berlin ☎ (030) 2173680 **○** Fri.–Sat. from 9pm *A favorite haunt for Germans and tourists alike. At the Loft you will be treated to the very latest sounds. At the Metropol, disco rules supreme.*

attracts big international names, is proof that a passion for jazz is shared by one and all.

From live music to improvisations, small jazz clubs to large concert halls.

## Basic facts

Berlin is without a doubt the *Kneipen* capital of Germany: there are more than 7000 of these traditional bistros in the city. With cafés open until dawn, countless bars, beer gardens and the *Kneipen*, Berlin is perfect for night owls. Here bars often stay open well past 1am, the usual

# After dark

### Restauration 1900 (36)
**Husemannstraße 1, 10435 Berlin ☎ (030) 4494052**

Ⓜ *Senefelder Platz* 🕐 *daily 11–1am* 🎴

A friendly *Kneipe*, in keeping with the other nearby turn-of-the-century buildings that are in the process of being restored. Inside, the decor is a mixture of the Industrial Revolution and modern chrome designs. This part of town is particularly popular during the summer months when the restaurants and *Kneipen* open their terraces to tourists and Berliners alike.

### Bar am Lützowplatz (37)
**Lützowplatz 7, 10785 Berlin ☎ (030) 2626807**

Ⓜ *Nollendorfplatz* 🕐 *daily 5pm–4am* 🍸

If you turn up after midnight, you'll be hard pushed to find a place at the longest bar in Berlin, which dominates the center of the room. Delicious cocktails, a wide selection of malt whiskies, and pleasant background music await this bar's customers, mainly residents from the Grand Hotel Esplanade ➡ 20 and people from the media and fashion worlds.

### Zur weißen Maus (38)
**Ludwigkirchplatz 12, 10719 Berlin ☎ (030) 8822264**

Ⓜ *Uhlandstraße* 🕐 *daily 9pm–4am* 🍸

Prints of Otto Dix paintings on the walls, mood lighting, and period music help to re-create a 1920s atmosphere at 'The White Mouse.' If you arrive after midnight, just ring the bell!

### Diener (39)
**Grolmanstraße 47, 10623 Berlin ☎ (030) 8815329**

Ⓜ *Uhlandstraße* 🕐 *daily 6pm –2am* 🎴 🍸

This former haunt of boxers (named after one of them) has become a Berlin institution. Inside you will find a smoky atmosphere and furniture that has seen better days – but it is a friendly bar and the ladies room, with its complimentary eau-de-Cologne and hair lacquer, is worth a visit! Frequented by stars and artists who come to see and be seen.

## Not forgetting

■ **Zeo Bar (40)** Rosenthaler Straße 40–41 (Hackesche Höfe, Hof I), 10178 Berlin *New, simple and elegant, in the Hackeschen Höfen* ➡ 86.
■ **Pinguin Club (41)** Wartburgstraße 54, 10823 Berlin ☎ (030) 7813005 *Kitsch 1950s decor. Frequented by journalists. A word of warning: the place gets packed later on.*
■ **Fogo (42)** Arndtstraße 29, 10965 Berlin ☎ (030) 6921465 *Brazilian bar with music from Latino groups.*
■ **Künstlerclub Die Möwe (43)** Am Festungsgraben 1, 10117 Berlin ☎ (030) 2823065 / 2824078 *A favorite haunt of artists, this traditional club has recently been renovated.*

# Bars and Kneipen

closing time in the rest of the country.

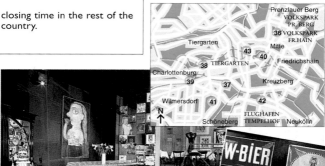

Photos and autographs of stars adorn the walls of the Diener.

## Basic facts

If you want to go dancing, Berlin is the perfect place. The city can cater for all tastes, from discos in the West to the 'techno temples' in the East. Once, you would have had to head for the Ku'damm to strut your stuff, but since reunification, clubs have opened in the elegant district of Mitte

# After dark

### Orpheo/San Fedele Pianobar (44)
**Uhlandstraße 19, 10623 Berlin ☎ (030) 8860782**

M *Uhlandstraße* ◯ *daily from 11pm*

At the beginning of the 1990s, this was a trendy club in the Ku'damm area. It has since relocated to new premises, where two bars mean shorter lines for drinks. A dance club for those into rhythm and blues, soul and disco music. Don't miss the performances by go-go dancers on weekends.

### Far Out (45)
**Kurfürstendamm 156, 10709 Berlin ☎ (030) 32000723**

M *Adenauerplatz* ◯ *Tue.–Sun. from 10pm*

This club has been popular for years. There is no particular dress code and the music suits all tastes, from party music and tango to funk and 1970s classics. From time to time, the club even holds non-smoking events!

### Delicious Doughnuts (46)
**Rosenthalerstraße 9, 10119 Berlin ☎ (030) 2833021**

M *Rosenthaler Platz* ◯ *daily 10pm–5am* 🎵

The Delicious Doughnuts is surrounded by bars and *Kneipen*. The establishment itself has a café in the front with a dance floor in the back. Those who manage to get past the female bouncer can enjoy acid, trip-hop, and jungle music. The club also hosts special house music nights and the occasional live performance.

### E-Werk (47)
**Wilhelmstraße 43, 10963 Berlin ☎ (030) 6179370**

M *Potsdamer Platz* ◯ *Sat. from midnight*

This psychedelic temple of techno has been opened, somewhat appropriately, in a former power station. It attracts DJs from around the world who come to play house, techno, trance, and acid music, so don't be put off by the lines waiting to get in!

## Not forgetting

■ **Blue Note Bar (48)** Courbièrestraße 13, 10787 Berlin
☎ (030) 2187248 *The clientele here tend to be very well dressed. Smart attire will make it easier to get past the bouncer. More than 100 cocktails to choose from, each as tasty as the next.*

■ **Tresor/Globus (49)** Leipziger Straße 126a, 10117 Berlin
☎ (030) 6093702 *Situated in the neighborhood once inhabited by the ministers of the Third Reich. Two dance floors: downstairs, in the former strongroom of the Karstadt department store, enjoy the best of techno and disco music. Upstairs, at Globus, it's house music. Go in the summer, when there is an open-air bar and barbecue.*

(the historical center of the city) and the trendy area of Prenzlauer Berg (formerly in East Berlin).

45

44

46

46

44

47

# What to see

## Concessions

If you're under 18, a student or over 60, you can benefit from reductions of up to 50% on the price of entrance to museums and galleries. State-run museums are free to everyone on the first Sunday of each month.

## Info-Box: a mine of information

The red Info-Box has become a symbol of the urban renewal currently taking place in the city, particularly around the Potsdamer Platz. It is full of information on the latest developments and can also be consulted via the Internet @ www.berlin.de

## Closed for renovations

The repercussions of German reunification have been felt not only in the political life of the country, but also in the way its cultural institutions are run. Many of Berlin's museums and galleries are undergoing extensive renovation work, which is unlikely to be completed before the end of the century. Be prepared for unexpected closures.

# 52
# Sights
THE INSIDER'S FAVORITES

## Berlin by bus

The No. 100 bus ➡ 15 will take you on a complete tour of the city's most famous monuments, from the Bahnhof Zoologischer Garten to the Alexanderplatz. The tour takes about an hour.

## Berlin by boat

If the weather is nice, why not enjoy a tour of Berlin's canals and waterways? For further information:
*Reederei Heinz Riedel, Planufer 78*
☎ *(030) 6934646*

## In the area

The Brandenburg Gate, dominating the Pariser Platz, is a symbol both of Berlin and of the events of 1989, and is a must for any visitor to the city. Now that the scaffolding and cranes have gone, the monument can once again be admired in all its glory. In October each year, the Berlin

# What to see

### Brandenburg Gate (1)
**Pariser Platz, 10117 Berlin (Mitte)**

🅜 *Unter den Linden*

The Brandenburg Gate (Brandenburger Tor) is the ultimate symbol of Berlin and of German reunification. It was opened in 1788 by Carl Gotthard Langhaus in the wall that then surrounded the city, following the course of the Spree River. The gate was intended to mark the beginning of the avenue Unter den Linden and serve as the main entrance to the city. The design of its impressive classical portico (128 feet long, 36 wide and 85 feet high) was based on the Propylea of the Acropolis in Athens. It was crowned in 1793 by Johan Gottfried Schadow's copper sculpture *Quadriga* (which was destroyed by bombs during World War II and later replaced by a copy). When the Berlin Wall was built, the Brandenburg Gate ended up in the East and became inaccessible to tourists until it was reopened on December 22, 1989, following the fall of the Communist government. The Gate dominates the Pariser Platz, once the home of nobles. Today, its neoclassical buildings are being extensively renovated; the Adlon Berlin hotel ➡ 18 has already been restored to its former glory, as has the former home of the German expressionist painter, Max Liebermann.

### Reichstagsgebäude (2)
**Platz der Republik, 10557 Berlin (Tiergarten) ☎ (030) 22732131**

🅜 *Unter den Linden* 🕒 *closed until the year 2000 for restoration*

The Reichstag (built in 1894 to a design by Paul Wallot) was the site of many important events in German history. It was from the balcony that Philipp Scheidemann, the Social-Democrat leader, proclaimed the Weimar Republic in 1918. In 1933, the fire that destroyed the dome and main chamber gave Hitler the excuse he needed to declare a state of emergency and ban the Communist party. In 1945, the victorious Soviet army flew its flag from the roof. In 1995, it was 'wrapped' by the artist Christo and his wife, Jeanne-Claude, a short-lived work of art that captured the attention of the entire world. The building is now undergoing extensive restoration work due to be completed by the year 2000, when the building will once again house the German parliament (the Bundestag).

### Hamburger Bahnhof (3)
**Invalidenstraße 50–51, 10557 Berlin (Tiergarten) ☎ (030) 3978340**

🅜 *Lehrter Stadtbahnhof* 🕒 *Tue.–Fri. 9am–5pm; Sat.–Sun. 10am–5pm*
● *DM8; concessions DM4; free on first Sun. of every month*

In 1996, the Berlin Museum of Modern Art (Museum für Gegenwart Berlin) was opened in the oldest and best preserved 19th-century railroad station in the city. Its entrance hall served as the model for many other German stations and is well worth a visit, as is the concourse built entirely in iron. The museum itself holds a collection of art spanning the past 30 years, including works by Anselm Kiefer and Andy Warhol.

# Pariser Platz/Invalidenstraße

Marathon begins at the Gate.
- ■ Where to stay ➜ 18
- ■ Where to shop ➜ 128

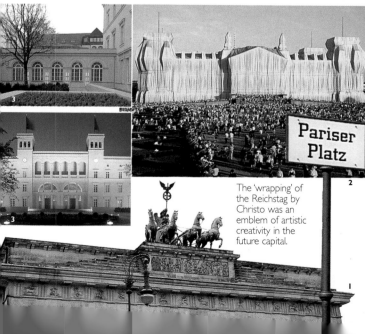

The 'wrapping' of the Reichstag by Christo was an emblem of artistic creativity in the future capital.

Pariser Platz

## In the area

A stroll along Unter den Linden will give you an impression of the grandeur of Prussia during the reign of Frederick the Great. The royal and imperial palaces, along with stately 19th-century buildings, bear witness to this sumptuous past. ■ Where to stay ➡ 28 ■ Where to

# What to see

## Unter den Linden (4)
### 10117 Berlin (Mitte)

Ⓜ *Unter den Linden*

For more than 400 years, the avenue 'Under the Limes' has been the most famous avenue in Berlin. Originally used as the approach to the palace in 1575, it was the setting for great pomp and ceremony during the reigns of the Prussian kings and the Kaisers. In their own times, the Nazis and the Communists recognized its symbolic value. As you walk along under the lime trees (replanted this century) keep an eye out for the former Soviet Embassy, the National Library, the statue of Frederick II and the palace of Wilhelm I.

## Forum Fridericianum (5)
### Unter den Linden/Bebelplatz, 10117 Berlin (Mitte)

Ⓜ *Französische Straße*

This square was designed for Frederick the Great by the architect Georg Wenceslas von Knobelsdorff. Of particular note are the Royal Library (1755), Humboldt University (1748), which numbers among its former students Marx and Engels, the Staatsoper ➡ 60, and St. Hedwige's Cathedral, modeled on the Pantheon in Rome.

## Gendarmenmarkt (6)
### Gendarmenmarkt, 10117 Berlin (Mitte)

Ⓜ *Hausvogteiplatz, Stadtmitte* **French cathedral** ☎ *(030) 2041506* 🕐 *Tue.–Sun. noon–5pm* ● *free* 🔲 *Sun. 11am–5pm* **German cathedral** ☎ *(030) 22732141 Tue.–Sun. 10am–7pm* ● *free* 🔲 *11am, 1pm, or by appointment*

The Gendarmenmarkt takes its name from an infantry regiment that was housed here in the 18th century. Overlooking the square is the Konzerthaus ➡ 60, the Französischer Dom or French cathedral (1701–1705), built for Huguenot refugees and now housing a Huguenot museum, and its German counterpart, the Deutscher Dom (1708).

## Friedrichwerdersche Kirche (7)
### Werderstraße, 10117 Berlin (Mitte) ☎ (030) 2081323

Ⓜ *Hausvogteiplatz* 🕐 *Tue.–Sun. 9am–5pm* ● *DM4; concessions DM2; free on first Sun. of every month*

Built between 1824 and 1830 by Karl Friedrich Schinkel in neo-Gothic style, the church now houses a museum dedicated to this Berlin architect. The exhibits include a fine collection of neoclassical sculptures.

## Not forgetting

■ **Neue Wache (8)** Unter den Linden 4, 10117 Berlin (Mitte) 🕐 *daily 10am–6pm Originally a guardhouse designed by Schinkel, now a monument to victims of fascism and militarism.*
■ **Deutsches Historisches Museum (9)** Unter den Linden 2, 10117 Berlin (Mitte) ☎ *(030) 215020* 🕐 *Mon.–Tue., Thur.–Sun. 10am–6pm Displays on German history in the former arsenal.*

## Unter den Linden  A B-C2 - G B-C4

eat ➡ 48 ■ After
dark ➡ 60 ➡ 62 ➡ 72
■ Where to shop
➡ 128 ➡ 130 ➡ 131

STAATS-
BIBLIOTHEK

Universitäts straße

11      30
31    8       43
H.d.Gießhs.
9

4  Unter den Linden

Friedrichstraße
Charlottenstraße

5        3
Bebel-  STAATS-
platz   OPER

Oberwallstraße

40

Niederlagstraße

Behrenstraße

41 25        39

7

Französische    Straße

M *Französische Str.*

22      2      42

Jägerstraße

26              6

Taubenstraße

M *Hausvogtei-
platz*

24          M *Stadtmitte*

Hausvogtei-
platz

N

Mohrenstraße

*Unter den Linden*

Unter den Linden is
lined with important
historic sites.

The Museumsinsel (Museum Island) occupies the northern end of a man-made island in the Spree. This complex of museums is remarkable for its sheer size, variety, and value. The exhibitions take the visitor on a journey through centuries of culture from around the world, from the

# What to see

10

11

12

12

## Altes Museum (10)
**Bodestraße 1–3, 10178 Berlin (Mitte)
☎ (030) 209050**

Ⓜ *Hackescher Markt* 🕐 *Tue., Thur.–Sun. 9am–5pm;
Wed. 9am–10pm for exhibitions ● DM12; concessions DM6*

The Old Museum was built in the style of a Greek temple – the cupola houses neoclassical sculptures of gods. The Lustgarten (pleasure garden) was originally designed as a park (1573) and later transformed into a parade ground. The enormous granite bowl, carved from a single piece of stone, is a masterpiece of the *Biedermeier* style.

## Alte Nationalgalerie (11)
**Bodestraße 1–3, 10178 Berlin (Mitte) ☎ (030) 209050**

Ⓜ *Hackescher Markt* 🕐 *Tue.–Sun. 9am–5pm ● DM4; concessions DM2*

The Old National Gallery houses paintings and sculptures from the 19th century to the beginning of the 20th century, including notable works by realist and impressionist painters, including Adolf Menzel, Max Liebermann and Arnold Böcklin.

## Pergamon-Museum (12)
**Bodestraße 1–3, 10178 Berlin (Mitte) ☎ (030) 209050**

Ⓜ *Hackescher Markt* 🕐 *Tue.–Sun. 9am–5pm ● DM4*

The Pergamon is the jewel of Berlin's museums, housing one of the largest and most astonishing collections of Greco-Roman antiquities in

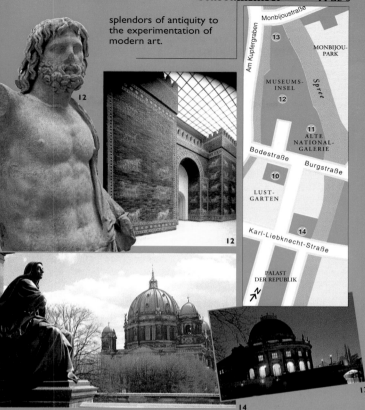

splendors of antiquity to the experimentation of modern art.

the world. Of particular note are the reconstructed ruins from ancient cities, such as the massive Pergamon altar from a Greek settlement in the eastern Aegean, and the treasures excavated by Heinrich Schliemann at Troy.

## Bode-Museum (13)
### Am Krupfergraben/Ingresso Monbijoubrücke, 10178 Berlin (Mitte) ☎ (030) 209050

Ⓜ *Hackescher Markt* 🕐 *Tue.–Sun. 9am–5pm* ● *DM4; concessions DM2; free on first Sun. of each month*

The gallery traces the development of German, Italian and Dutch art from the 13th century to the 18th century. Of particular interest among the sculptures are the late-Gothic and Italian statues.

## Berliner Dom (14)
### Lustgarten, 10178 Berlin (Mitte) ☎ (030) 20269136

Ⓜ *Hackescher Markt* 🕐 *11.30am–6pm* **Crypt** *Mon.–Sat. 9am–6pm; Sun. 11.30am–6pm* ● *DM5; under-14s free*

This cathedral and pantheon of the Hohenzollern family, which ruled Berlin for more than 500 years, was built between 1894 and 1905. Based on St. Peter's in Rome, it is typical of imperial architecture. Of particular note: the loggia of Kaiser Wilhelm II, the baptismal fonts, and the altar. The crypt, now a museum, holds the tombs of the Hohenzollern family.

## In the area

The area stretching from the Alexanderplatz to the Nikolaiviertel is the original heart of Berlin. As you stroll past medieval churches, rococo palaces, and concrete buildings of the Communist era, the history of Berlin will unfold before your eyes. ■ Where to stay ➡ 30

# What to see

### Alexanderplatz (15)
**Panoramastraße/Alexanderplatz, 10178 Berlin (Mitte)**

Ⓜ *Alexanderplatz* **Television tower** 🕙 *daily 9–1am* ☎ *(030) 2423333*
● *DM8; concessions DM4* 🔄

In the 1920s, the Alexanderplatz was one of the city's major thoroughfares. The war and various rebuilding projects turned it into a monument of socialist architecture and the center of East Berlin. Today, its block-like concrete buildings are due to be replaced with modern skyscrapers. The television tower that dominates the square is the third-tallest building in Europe, and its revolving iron and glass dome offers a panoramic view over the city. On the southeast side of the square is the 19th-century Rotes Rathaus (the red city hall). This brick building is neo-Renaissance in style, with a tower that recalls London's Big Ben. On the second floor, 36 earthenware bas-reliefs recount the history of Berlin.

### Marienkirche (16)
**Karl-Liebknecht-Straße 8, 10178 Berlin (Mitte) ☎ (030) 2424467**

Ⓜ *Alexanderplatz* 🕙 *Mon.–Thur. 10am–noon, 1–5pm; Sat.–Sun. noon–4pm*
*Organ recitals May–Oct.: Sat. 4.30–5.30pm*

Visitors to St. Mary's, one of the few old churches on the east side of Berlin, should pay special attention to the *danse macabre* or dance of death (1484), an anonymous fresco depicting the great plague of 1480–84. Also of interest are the bronze fonts (1437), the baroque marble pulpit designed by Andreas Schlüter (1703) and the organ, played by Johann Sebastian Bach in 1747.

### Nikolaiviertel (17)
**Rathausstraße/Mühlendamm/Spandauer Straße
10178 Berlin (Mitte)**

Ⓜ *Alexanderplatz*

The district of St. Nicholas, with its cobbled streets, low buildings, craftsmen's studios and countless nooks and crannies, lies at the heart of Old Berlin. Many of the buildings, however, are not original, having been rebuilt in 1987 to mark the 750th anniversary of the city. Apart from St. Nicholas' church, the oldest parish church in Berlin (13th century), take time to visit the Ephraim-palais (no. 16 Poststraße), a group of 20 houses built between 1761 and 1764 and now displaying temporary exhibitions on Berlin-related topics, and the Knoblauchhaus (no. 23 Poststraße), a beautiful baroque residence from the end of the 18th century. The area is also home to a number of *Kneipen*, including the famous Zum Nussbaum (The Hazelnut Tree).

## Not forgetting

■ **Franziskaner Klosterkirche (18)** Klosterstraße/Grunerstraße, 10179 Berlin (Mitte) *This masterpiece of 14th-century Berlin Gothic architecture was formerly a high school attended by Otto von Bismark.*

## In the area

In the 1930s, the area north of the Alexanderplatz was the hidden face of Berlin. Here in the narrow streets, Eastern European Jews lived alongside the city's poor and the criminal underworld. Now, the area has been redeveloped and is newly fashionable. ■ Where to eat ➡ 50

# What to see

## Hackesche Höfe (19)
### Rosenthaler Straße 40–41, 10178 Berlin (Mitte)

Ⓜ *Hackescher Markt*

The Hackesche Höfe are ten buildings built around 1906 that have, for the most part, retained their *Jugendstil* (art nouveau) façades and colorful storefronts. These are now home to trendy clothing stores, bookstores, antiques stores, art galleries, *Kneipen,* and theaters.

## Neue Synagoge (20)
### Oranienburger Straße 28–30, 10117 Berlin (Mitte)
### ☎ (030) 2801250

Ⓜ *Oranienburger Straße* 🕙 *Mon.–Thur. 10am–6pm; Fri. 10am–2pm* ● *DM5; concessions DM3*

The New Synagogue was built between 1859 and 1866, following a Moorish-Byzantine design and crowned with a golden dome. On November 9, 1938, or Kristallnacht (the night of the broken glass), when the Nazis destroyed Jewish homes, stores, and synagogues, it was seriously damaged, then was completely destroyed by fire in 1943. Now rebuilt, the synagogue is the home of the Centrum Judaicum.

## Sophienstraße (21)
### Sophienstraße, 10178 Berlin (Mitte)

Ⓜ *Weinmeisterstraße*

This narrow, 19th-century street is lined with beautifully restored houses, small boutiques, and fine old *Kneipen*. St. Sophie's church has the last remaining baroque bell tower in Berlin.

## Kulturzentrum Tacheles (22)
### Oranienburger Straße 54-56, 10117 Berlin (Mitte)
### ☎ (030) 2826185

Ⓜ *Oranienburger Tor, Oranienburger Straße*

The Tacheles cultural center was set up amid the ruins of what was once one of the city's largest stores. There are exhibits in a variety of media, including painting, sculpture, cinema, theater, and music. Nearby, antiques-hunters can browse the stalls of the flea market before stopping at one of the popular *Kneipen* on Oranienburger Straße.

## Not forgetting

■ **Alter Jüdischer Friedhof (23)** Große Hamburger Straße 26, 10115 Berlin (Mitte) *This was once the main street of the Jewish community. At no. 27, in the old primary school, you can find reminders of the 55,000 Jews who were sent to the camps at Auschwitz and Theresienstaad. On the site of the old Jewish cemetery, in use from the 17th century until it was desecrated by the Nazis during Kristallnacht, there is a copy of the tomb of the illuminist philosopher, Moses Mendelssohn (1729–86).*

■ After
dark ➡ 64
➡ 66 ➡ 72

## In the area

The landmarks between the Potsdamer Platz and Checkpoint Charlie present a chronicle of Berlin's 20th-century history. Some places recall the 1920s, others offer reminders of the horrors of the Nazi dictatorship and the building of the 'wall of hate', while still others bear

# What to see

### Potsdamer Platz and Leipziger Platz (24)
#### Potsdamer Platz, 10785 Berlin (Tiergarten)

M *Potsdamer Platz* **Info-Box** *Leipziger Platz 21* ☉ *Mon.–Wed., Fri.–Sun. 9am–7pm; Thur. 9am–9pm* ● *free.* **Views over Berlin** *Mon.–Wed., Fri.–Sun. 9am–7pm; Thur. 9am–9pm; closed when there is snow or ice on the ground* ● *DM2* ♿

During the 1920s, the Potsdamer Platz was the busiest crossroads in Europe. Following the war and the building of the Wall, the area was eerily deserted. Today it is the biggest building site in the world. Supervised by the Italian architect Renzo Piano and others, many offices, homes, cultural institutes, and stores are currently being built.

### Preußischer Landtag (25)
#### Niederkirchnerstraße 3–5, 10117 Berlin (Mitte) ☎ (030) 23250

M *Potsdamer Platz* ☉ *Mon.–Fri. 9am–6pm*

Once home to the Prussian parliament and now the seat of Berlin's regional parliament, this building has played many roles in the city's history. In 1918, it was the scene of meetings between the workers and the military. In 1936, it became Goering's Haus des Fliegers (Airmen's hostel) and under the Communist regime, it was the Prime Minister's residence. The adjoining building housed the Nazi Ministry of Aviation and is the headquarters of the Treuhand, the organization in charge of privatizations of former East German companies.

### Martin-Gropius-Bau (26)
#### Stresemannstraße 110, 10963 Berlin (Kreuzberg) ☎ (030) 254860

M *Potsdamer Platz, Anhalter Bahnhof* ☉ *daily 10am–8pm* ● *DM12; concessions DM6*

This is a popular venue for temporary exhibitions from the Berlinische Galerie, centered around the art and cultural history of Berlin from the 19th century to the present day.

24

24

witness to
reunification.
■ After dark ➡ 74

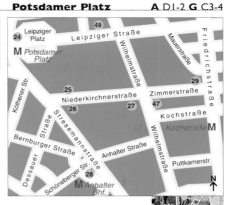

Leipziger
Platz
24
M Potsdamer
Platz
Leipziger Straße
49
Wilhelmstraße
Mauerstraße
Friedrichstraße
29
25
Köthener Str.
Niederkirchnerstraße
Zimmerstraße
26
27
47
Kochstraße
Stresemannstraße
Kochstraße M
Bernburger Straße
Anhalter Straße
Wilhelmstraße
Dessauer Straße
Schöneberger Str.
28
Puttkamerstr.
M Anhalter
Bhf.
N

The area around the
Potsdamer Platz and the
Leipziger Platz is the
scene of extensive
rebuilding work: the
'Berlin 2005' project is the
most ambitious urban
renewal scheme since the
end of the war.

## Prinz-Albrecht-Gelände (27)
### Stresemannstraße 110, 10963 Berlin (Kreuzberg)
### ☎ (030) 25486703

🕙 10am–6pm ● free

This collection of foundations is all that remains of the
Nazi Gestapo and SS headquarters. The area, with its
system of underground tunnels, has been renamed the
'topography of terror'. Don't miss the well-documented
exhibition.

## Not forgetting

■ **Anhalter Bahnhof (28)** Askanischer Platz, 10963
Berlin (Kreuzberg) *Ruins of what was the main train station.*
■ **Checkpoint Charlie (29)** Friedrichstraße/
Zimmerstraße, 10963 *The site of the first confrontation
between American and Soviet tanks (1961). The exhibition on
the history of the Wall is a must.*

29

24

24

## In the area

The Tiergarten was formerly the hunting ground for the rulers of Prussia and is now the city's main area of parkland. To the south is the eerie embassy quarter, built by the Nazis, deserted since the end of the war and now in ruins and overrun with weeds.

# What to see

### Tiergarten (30)
**Straße des 17. Juni, 10785 Berlin (Tiergarten)**

M *Tiergarten, Bellevue*

Five hundred acres of greenery in the heart of the city, criss-crossed by 15 miles of paths that take the visitor past lawns, lakes, flowerbeds, and playgrounds, the Tiergarten is a site of great beauty and much history. The park was severely damaged during the harsh winter of 1946, when Berliners were driven to cutting down the trees for firewood and planting potatoes and beets along the paths. It was restored following the war, the work funded by donations from West German towns. The Avenue of 17 June, named after the revolt by East Berliners against the Soviet regime that took place in 1953, crosses the park, linking the Stadtschloß to Charlottenburg Schloss. It was widened in 1938 by Albert Speer so that it could be used for military parades. The park also has a café on stilts, boats for hire and, at the weekend, the largest flea market in Berlin ➡ 130.

### Schloß Bellevue (31)
**Spreeweg 1, 10557 Berlin (Tiergarten) ☎ (030) 390840**

M *Bellevue*

This French baroque-style palace was built in 1785 as a summer house for the youngest brother of Frederick the Great and was owned by the ruling Hohenzollern family until 1918. Badly damaged during the last war, it has since been rebuilt and is now the official residence of the German President. Only the oval salon remains of the original building. Before the ravages of war, the palace's grounds, some 50 acres in total, were considered to be among the finest in the city.

### Siegessäule (32)
**Straße des 17. Juni am Großen Stern, 10785 Berlin (Tiergarten) ☎ (030) 3912961**

M *Ernst-Reuter-Platz, Zoologischer Garten* ⬤ *Mon. 1–6pm; Tue.–Sun. 9am–6pm; closed when there is snow or ice on the ground* ● *DM2; concessions DM1*

The Victory Column (1864–73) was erected at the request of Kaiser Wilhelm I to commemorate Prussia's victory over France and Denmark. The huge, gold-covered statue of the goddess of victory stood in front of the Reichstag until 1938. Those who brave the 285 steps that spiral up the column are rewarded with a wonderful view over the Tiergarten and much of Berlin.

## Not forgetting

■ **Haus der Kulturen der Welt (33)** John-Foster-Dulles-Allee 10, 10557 Berlin (Tiergarten) ☎ (030) 397870 / 39787178 ⬤ *Tue.–Sun. 10am–8pm The World Culture Center is an important venue for conferences, exhibitions and concerts. The building itself was a gift from the United States for the international architecture fair of 1957. Its curved roof and yawning façade have earned the building the nickname of 'the pregnant oyster'. In front, in the fountain, stands a bronze statue by Henry Moore.*

■ Where
to shop
➡ 130

## In the area

The Kulturforum, not far from the Potsdamer Platz, is one of the city's major cultural centers. Collections previously scattered throughout East and West Berlin are being brought together in this interesting museum complex. ■ Where to stay ➡ 20 ■ Where to eat ➡ 44

# What to see

## Kulturforum (34)
### Between Tiergartenstraße and Potsdamer Straße, 10785 Berlin (Tiergarten)

Ⓜ *Potsdamer Platz* 🕓 *Tue.–Fri. 9am–5pm; Sat.–Sun. 10am–5pm* **Handicrafts Museum** *Matthäikirchstraße 10* ☎ *(030) 2662911* ● *DM4; concessions DM2; free on first Sun. of every month.* **Musical Instruments Museum** *Tiergartenstraße 1* ☎ *(030) 254810* ● *DM4; concessions DM2; free on first Sun. of every month.* **Drawings and Prints Room** *Matthäikirchplatz 4* 🕓 *Tue.–Fri. 9am–4pm* ☎ *(030) 2662002* ● *free*

The Drawings and Prints Room houses an impressive collection from the Middle Ages to the present day. Of note in the Handicrafts Museum are the treasures of the Guelphs (11th–15th centuries) and the 18th-century transformable table. The Musical Instrument Museum takes the visitor on a journey through 400 years of musical history.

## Neue Nationalgalerie (35)
### Potsdamer Straße 50, 10785 Berlin (Tiergarten)
### ☎ (030) 2662662

Ⓜ *Potsdamer Platz* 🕓 *Tue.–Fri. 9am–5pm; Sat.–Sun. 10am–5pm* ● *DM4; concessions DM2; free on first Sun. of every month*

This glass and steel structure (1965–68) was the last project of Mies van der Rohe, the leading Bauhaus architect. It is the home of the new National Gallery, which specializes in 20th-century art, with fine collections of Bauhaus, expressionist, and surrealist works.

■ After
dark ➡ 60

## Bauhaus-Archiv (36)
### Klingelhöferstraße 14, 10785 Berlin (Tiergarten) ☎ (030) 2540020

Ⓜ *Wittenbergplatz* 🕐 *Mon.,Wed.–Sun. 10am–5pm* ● *DM5; concessions DM2.50; free on Mon.*

The archive displays a collection of architectural models, projects, paintings, and designs by some of the leading exponents of Bauhaus, including van der Rohe, Schlemmer and Breuer.

## Gedenkstätte Deutscher Winderstand (37)
### Stauffenbergstraße 13–14, 10785 Berlin (Tiergarten) ☎ (030) 26542202 / 26542213

Ⓜ *Potsdamer Platz* 🕐 *9am–6pm; Sat.–Sun. 9am–1pm* ● *free*

In the courtyard of the former Nazi army headquarters, there is a plaque in memory of four officers of the Wehrmacht who were sentenced to death after a failed attempt on the life of Hitler. On the third floor is a museum dedicated to the German resistance.

### Not forgetting

■ **Staatsbibliothek zu Berlin (38)** Potsdamer Straße 33, 10785 Berlin (Tiergarten) ☎ (030) 2661 *Built between 1967 and 1978 by Hans Scharoun, this is one of the largest libraries in Europe, with some eight million volumes, including original texts by Hegel, Herder and Fichte.*

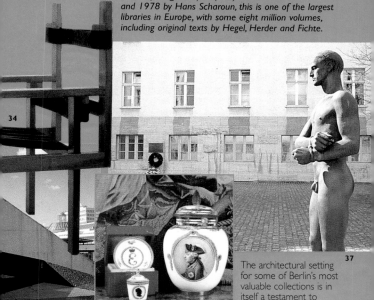

The architectural setting for some of Berlin's most valuable collections is in itself a testament to modern design.

The Kurfürstendamm, known by all as the "Ku'Damm", is the main avenue in the western part of the city, and the surrounding area is a hive of activity. ■ Where to stay ➡ 20 ➡ 22 ➡ 24 ➡ 25 ➡ 26 ■ Where to eat ➡ 34 ➡ 38 ■ After dark ➡ 64 ➡ 66 ➡ 68 ➡ 70 ➡ 74

# What to see

### Kurfürstendamm (39)
#### Berlin (Charlottenburg/Wilmersdorf)

🅜 *Kurfürstendamm, Uhlandstraße*

Stretching for more than two miles, the Kurfürstendamm was originally little more than a bridle path, used by the family of the Prussian ruler to get to and from their hunting lodge in Grunewald. It was transformed in 1883 when the Chancellor, Otto von Bismark, constructed a boulevard worthy of the capital of the German empire, inspired by the splendor of the Champs-Élysées in Paris. It quickly became one of the city's main thoroughfares. Many cabarets, variety clubs, and movie theaters opened during the 1920s. Today there is little left of the original avenue which suffered greatly during the war. It is still, however, a lively street, with its expensive stores, relaxing cafés (try the Kranzler), and theaters and cinemas. Breitscheidplatz, with its pink granite globe fountain, is one of the city's main meeting places.

### Kaiser-Wilhelm-Gedächtniskirche (40)
#### Breitscheidplatz, 10789 Berlin (Charlottenburg) ☎ (030) 2185023

🅜 *Zoologischer Garten* 🕑 *daily 9am–7pm* ● *free*

The Memorial Church was built in 1895 by Wilhelm II in honor of his grandfather, Kaiser Wilhelm I. The building was destroyed in 1943, leaving only the west tower standing. Through public demand, restoration work began at the beginning of the 1960s. The architect Egon Eiermann integrated the remains into a new church, an octagonal structure with stained-glass façades and a second tower. On the hour every hour, the bell in the old tower, known as the 'hollow tooth', rings out a tune composed by Louis Ferdinand, great-grandson of the last emperor.

### Zoologischer Garten (41)
#### Budapester Straße 34, 10787 Berlin (Tiergarten) ☎ (030) 254010

🅜 *Zoologischer Garten* **Zoological gardens** 🕑 *winter: 9am–dusk; summer: 9am–6.30pm* ● *DM11; children (3–15) DM5.5* **Aquarium** *Budapester Straße 32* ☎ *(030) 254010* 🕑 *daily 9am–6pm* ● *DM11; children (3–15) DM5.5* **Zoological gardens and aquarium** ● *DM18; children (3–15) DM8*

This zoological garden covering more than 80 acres was opened in 1844 in the grounds of the royal pheasant farm. Today it is one of the largest zoos in the world with more than 14,000 animals and almost 1400 different species. Of particular note are the aviary and aquarium.

## Not forgetting

■ **Käthe-Kollwitz-Museum (42)** Fasanenstraße 24, 10719 Berlin (Charlottenburg) ☎ (030) 8825210 ● *DM8; concessions half price. This museum, located in a small palace, boasts a large collection of the expressionist's work, including 100 engravings and 70 drawings.*

■ Where
to shop
➡ 120

41

39

39

39

40

39

41

## In the area

The palace of the Hohenzollerns thankfully escaped the war intact and remains a jewel of Prussian baroque architecture. It is a must for visitors interested in architecture and equally enjoyable for those who simply want to stroll around the grounds and explore the surrounding area,

# What to see

### Schloß Charlottenburg (43)
**Spandauer Damm/Luisenplatz, 10585 Berlin (Charlottenburg)**
**☎ (030) 320911**

Ⓜ *Richard-Wagner-Platz* 🕐 *Tue.–Fri. 9am–5pm; Sat.–Sun. 10am–5pm* ● *day pass DM15* 🎫 *DM8 Ala Knobelsdorff* ● *DM3 Galerie der Romantik* ● *DM4; free on first Sun. of every month*

In 1695, Elector Frederick III had this summer residence built for his wife, Sophie Charlotte. The east wing was built by Frederick the Great, and Frederick-Wilhelm II added a theater to the west wing. This theater now houses the Museum of Prehistory and Protohistory. The porcelain room, the apartments of Frederick the Great, the rococo style Golden Gallery and the Romantics Gallery (with paintings by Caspar David Friedrich) have been meticulously restored.

### Schloßpark Charlottenburg (44)
**Spandauer Damm/Luisenplatz, 10585 Berlin (Charlottenburg)**

Ⓜ *Richard-Wagner-Platz* 🕐 *Tue.–Fri. 9am–5pm; Sat.–Sun. 10am–5pm* ● *free Mauseleum summer only Summer house and tea house ☎ (030) 32091285 Tue.–Fri. 11am–3pm; Sat.–Sun. 10am–3pm Schinkel Pavilion ☎ (030) 32091212 Tue.–Sun. 10am–5pm*

Originally designed in 1687 as a French baroque garden, the grounds were transformed into an English-style garden at the beginning of the 19th century. Of particular interest are the elegant gazebo, designed as a teahouse, and the marble tomb of Queen Luise and Wilhelm I. A collection of *Biedermeier* ornaments are on display in the pavilion designed by Schinkel in the style of a Neapolitan villa.

with its atmosphere
of Old Berlin.
■ Where to eat
➡ 42

SCHLOßPARK
CHARLOTTENBURG

43

Bonhoefferufer
Spree
Sommerringstraße
Charlottenburger Ufer
Luisen-
platz
Eosanderstraße
Winterfeldstraße
Spandauer Damm
44
Brauhofstraße
45
Otto-Suhr-Allee
46
Nithackstraße
Kaiser-Friedrich-Straße
29
Schloßstraße
Gierke-
platz
Schustehrusstr.
Richard-Wagner- M N
Platz
28

43

## Ägyptisches Museum (45)
### Schloßstraße 70, 14059 Berlin (Charlottenburg) ☎ (030) 320911

Ⓜ *Richard-Wagner-Platz* Ⓠ *Tue.–Fri. 9am–5pm; Sat.–Sun. 10am–5pm* ● *DM8;
concessions DM4; free on first Sun. of every month*

The Egyptian Museum is opposite the palace in the former officers' mess
for the Royal Guard. Among the famous pieces in the impressive
collection are the polychrome bust of Nefertiti and the Kalabsha Gate
(around 20 BC). Everyday objects, ceramics, papyruses, pieces of
parchment, wooden and wax tablets, and various other treasures offer
the visitor a fascinating overview of the culture of Ancient Egypt.

## Bröhan-Museum (46)
### Schloßstraße 1a, 14059 Berlin (Charlottenburg) ☎ (030) 3214029

Ⓜ *Richard-Wagner-Platz* Ⓠ *Tue.–Sun. 10am–6pm* ● *DM6; concessions DM3*

Housed in a former infantry barracks (1893), this small museum is
devoted to the *Jugendstil* and art deco movements. The collection
includes china, furniture, and paintings, as well as drawings and engravings
by Max Liebermann and Lovis Corinth.

This limestone bust of
Queen Nefertiti,
hauntingly lifelike and
beautiful, is one of
the most famous
pieces in
Berlin's
Egyptian
Museum.

44

45

45

## In the area

Dahlem is a residential area with many beautiful parks and even some remaining areas of farmland. Berliners pride themselves on its Free University (famous for its scientific research) and its large museum complex, a veritable treasure trove.

# What to see

## Botanischer Garten (47)
### Königin-Luise-Straße 6–8, 14195 Berlin (Steglitz)
### ☎ (030) 83006127

**M** *Botanischer Garten* **Gardens** 🕒 *Nov.–Jan.: 9am–4pm; Feb. 9am–5pm; Mar., Oct.: 9am–6pm; Apr., Aug.–Sep.: 9am–8pm; May–July 9am–9pm; Sat.–Sun. from 10am* **Greenhouses** *Close 1 hour before the gardens* **Museum** *Tue.–Sun. 10am–5pm* ● *DM6; concessions DM3*

Built between 1897 and 1903, this is the largest botanical garden in Europe, covering some 100 acres and containing more than 18,000 different plants and trees. Don't miss the Prince's Garden, where some of the plants date back to the 17th century, the scented garden, the 'garden of flavors', the collection of more than 1800 different species of tree, or the 18 greenhouses with their carnivorous plants, palms, and orchids. The large tropical greenhouse shelters giant bamboo.

## Museum Dahlem (48)
### Arnimallee/Lansstraße, 14195 Berlin (Zehlendorf) ☎ (030) 83011

**M** *Dahlem-Dorf* 🕒 *Tue.–Fri. 9am–5pm; Sat.–Sun. 10am–5pm* **Picture Gallery** *Arnimallee 23–27* ● *DM4; concessions DM2; free on first Sun. of every month* **Museum of Indian Art, Museum of Islamic Art, Museum of East Asian Art, Ethnological Museum** *Lansstraße 8* ● *DM4; concessions DM2* **Museum of Early Christian and Byzantine Art** *Arnimallee 23–27* ● *DM4; concessions DM2; free on first Sun. of every month*

Any stay in Berlin must include a visit to this vast museum complex. With more than 600 canvases dating from the 13th to the 18th centuries, the Picture Gallery is one of the largest collections of Western art in the world: you can admire works by Giotto, Mantegna, Botticelli, Raphael, Titian, Vermeer, Rubens, El Greco, Watteau, and Gainsborough, as well as 21 paintings by Rembrandt. The Museum of Indian Art is the home of the Turfan collections from the mountains of Tibet and bronze statues of the god Vishnu, cast in Pakistan in the 7th century. In the Ethnological Museum, 453,000 exhibits document far-off civilizations. The Museum of Early Christian and Byzantine Art houses many ivory statues and icons.

## Domäne Dahlem (49)
### Königin-Luise-Straße 49, 14195 Berlin (Zehlendorf)
### ☎ (030) 8325000

**M** *Dahlem-Dorf* 🕒 *Mon., Tue.–Sun. 10am–6pm* ● *DM3; concessions DM1.50*

The old neighborhood of Dahlem-Dorf (Dahlem Village) has existed since at least the 13th century. The attractive village church dates from 1220 and contains a 15th-century altar. The manor house contains a small museum dedicated to the history of the village, which was an independent fief in the 17th and 18th centuries, only being sold to the state at the beginning of the 19th century. Dahlem holds an organic market every Saturday and also organizes a number of entertaining fairs and festivals throughout the year.

**47**

**47**

The Tropical Greenhouse in the Botanical Garden is a real crystal palace

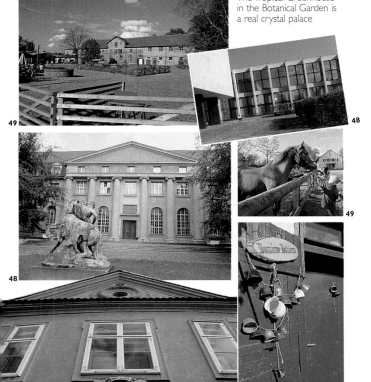

**49**

**48**

**49**

**48**

**49**

**48**

**49**

## In the area

This modern, dynamic part of the city hosts exhibitions, trade fairs, conferences, and major musicsl events. From the viewing gallery of the Funkturm (the radio tower) you can enjoy a spectacular view over West Berlin and the Grunewald forest.

# What to see

## Funkturm (50)
### Messedamm, 14057 Berlin (Charlottenburg)

🅼 *Kaiserdamm* **Viewing platform** 🕐 *daily 10am–11pm* ● *DM6; concessions DM3* ☎ *(030) 30382996 noon–3pm, 6–10pm* 🆚 **Museum of German Radio** *Hammarskjöldplatz 1* ☎ *(030) 3028186 Mon., Wed.–Sun. 10am–5pm* ● *DM3; concessions DM1.50*

The Funkturm radio tower, erected to mark the third German Radio Exhibition (1924–26), is one of the most famous and best-loved symbols of Berlin. When the tower was built, it was designed to be a radio transmitter, panoramic viewing tower (complete with a restaurant) and also a base for air traffic control. A few years later, in 1929, it was from here that the world's first television signals were transmitted. The corner pylons rest on porcelain bases, like old-fashioned insulators. At the foot of the tower is the Museum of Radio, reflecting the fact that Berlin led the world in pioneering early radio broadcasts – it was from the Voxhaus on Potsdamer Straße that the first ever radio broadcast in Germany was made.

## ICC/Messegelände (51)
### Hammarskjöldplatz, 14055 Berlin (Charlottenburg)
### ☎ (030) 30384444 Foires et congrès ☎ (030) 30383085

🅼 *Kaiserdamm, Theodor-Heuss-Platz* 🕐 *times vary* ● *prices vary*

The ICC/Messegelände is the largest exhibition and trade fair center in the world. The vast exhibition park comprises 25 exhibition halls. The complex is dominated by the ICC (International Congress Centrum), which is designed to resenble a large spaceship, with its façade covered with aluminum panels. It is the venue for events such as the International Exhibition of Radio and Television and numerous other national and international fairs and exhibitions. In front of the building is a large statue in steel by the French artist Jean-Robert Ipoustéguy, which represents Alexander the Great before Ecbatana. Although the complex existed before World War I, most of the buildings date from the 1930s to the present day. The center welcomes millions of visitors each year, with more than half a million passing through the turnstiles during Grüne Woche (Green week, the largest European trade fair of the agricultural and food sectors).

## Autodromo Avus (52)
### 14055 Berlin (Grunewald)

🅼 *Westkreuz*

Between the exhibition complex and the district of Nikolassee, the Grunewald park is crossed by the five-mile circuit of the Avus racetrack. It was on this track, back in 1926, that the first German Grand Prix took place – two world speed records were broken during the event. As the city has grown, the track has now become part of the city's freeway system and it is against the law to go any faster than 65mph! Nevertheless, from time to time, races are still held here in honour of its famous past.

**50**

**51**

**51**

**51**

**50**

The radio tower was a powerful symbol of the modern age when it was built in the 1920s.

# Further afield

**Organized trips**
The agencies organizing guided
tours of the city ➡ 15 also offer
bus and boat trips to the
surrounding areas.

## Around Berlin: the Brandenburg countryside

The area around Berlin, known as the Brandenburg countryside, is a highly varied landscape. Large sandy plains are dotted with pine, beech, and oak forests and interspersed with around 3000 lakes. In many of the small towns and villages, you can still come across attactive, well-preserved 12th and 13th-century red-brick churches.

# 25
# Days out
## THE INSIDER'S FAVORITES

## Visiting the areas around Berlin

Since reunification, it has become much easier to visit the countryside around Berlin, and some of the more popular destinations are now less than two hours away by bus or train. The train mainly serves areas to the east and if you want to head toward the southwest, follow a route toward Potsdam ➡ 112 (the capital of Brandenburg) and pick up a connection there. Renting a car ➡ 8 is obviously the most flexible way to visit the surrounding area. The freeways are in quite good condition, in spite of one or two roadworks, and there are no tolls. Best of all, gas is reasonably inexpensive.

# Further afield

Neuruppin

N.167

A24 ← Hamburg

## Pfaueninsel
(1–4) ➡ 106

🚌 (20 mins) A115 (Stadtautobahn Avus) heading southwest; N1 from Zehlendorf to Wannsee, then follow signs for the island.
Ⓜ S1, S3, S7 to Wannsee, then the 🚌 216 or the 316 as far as Moorlake or Pfaueninsel.
⛴ (10 mins) from the pier at Nikolskoer Weg.

A10

A111

Havel

Berliner Ring

A10

Berlin-Tegel ✈

BER

N.5

Bahnho Zoo

N.2

Havel

N273

Pfaueninsel

Tennis-Turnier-Club Rot-Weiß

Glienicke

Sanssouci

N.1

Potsdam

A115

A10

A2

← Magdeburg

A9

Berliner Ring

A10

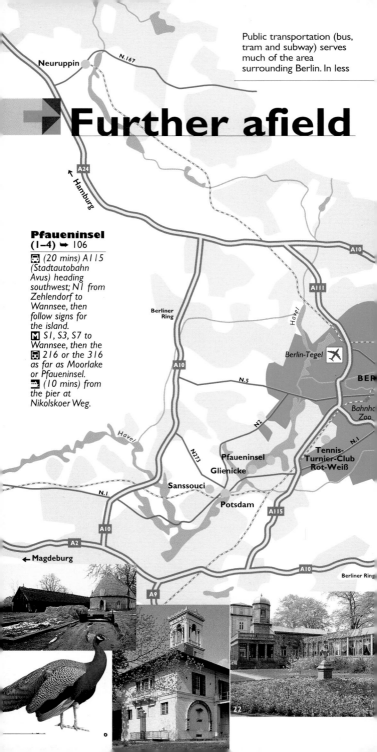

22

than an hour you can escape the bustle of city life and relax in the peace and quiet of the Brandenburg countryside, visiting one of its many sites of historical interest or going to one of the country clubs to enjoy a game of golf or tennis, or go horseback riding.

## Glienicke
**(5–9)** ➡ 108

🚗 (30 mins) A115 (Stadtautobahn Avus) heading southwest; N1 from Zehlendorf to Potsdam, then follow signposts for Glienicke
Ⓜ S1, S3, S7 to Wannsee, then 🚋 as far as Glienicker Brücke.

## Schloßpark Sanssouci
**(10–14)** ➡ 110

🚗 (35–40 mins) From Charlottenburg, take the N2. From Zehlendorf, take the A115 and the N1.
Ⓜ S3, S7 Potsdam Stadt, then 🚌 695 as far as 'An der historischen Mühle' ('The Historical Mill').

## Potsdam
**(15–18)** ➡ 112

🚗 (35–40 mins) From Charlottenburg, take the N2. From Zehldorf, take the A115 and the N1.
Ⓜ S3, S7 Potsdam, then 🚋 (tram) 92, 96 or 98 as far as the Platz der Einheit.

## Neuruppin
**(19–22)** ➡ 114

🚗 (50–60 mins) A24 toward Amburo-Rostock, exit Neuruppin, then take the B167 toward Neuruppin.
🏛 Zoological gardens
☎ Enquiries (03381) 534233

## Horseback riding
**(23)** ➡ 116

Galopprennbahn Hoppegarten
🚗 (50 mins) B115 heading toward Frankfurt an der Oder, then follow the signposts after Mahlsdorf

Ⓜ S5 heading toward Strausberg. Get off at Hoppegarten-Mark, then a 4-min walk.

## Golf
**(24)** ➡ 116

Sporting Club Berlin Scharmützelsee e.V.
🚗 (60 mins) Beltway A10 (Berliner Ring) heading toward Frankfurt an der Oder, exit Fürstenwalde, then take the road to Bad Saarow.

## Tennis
**(25)** ➡ 116

Tennis-Turnier-Club Rot-Weiß
🚗 (15–20 mins) A115, exit Hüttenweg
Ⓜ S3, S7 Grunewald, then 🚌 186 to the stop also called Grunewald, then a 5-min walk.

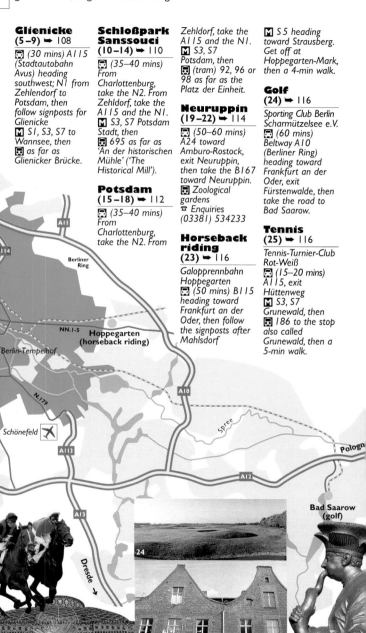

Berliner Ring

A11

A114

Berlin-Tempelhof

N.179

Hoppegarten (horseback riding)

NN.1-5

Schönefeld ✈

A113

A10

Spree

Polen

A12

A13

Dresden →

Bad Saarow (golf)

24

## Basic facts

Pfaueninsel (peacock island) owes its name to the regal birds that still add an air of exoticism to this island in the Havel. On discovering this haven of peace in 1793, Frederick-Wilhelm II had a small castle built here which he used for his illicit love affair with Wilhelmine von Encke.

# Further afield

### Schloß Pfaueninsel (1)
#### Nikolskoer Weg, Berlin (Zehlendorf) ☎ (030) 8053042

Ⓜ *Wannsee* Ⓒ *Castle Apr.–Oct. 10am–12.30pm, 1.30–4.30pm **Gardens** May–Aug. 8am–8pm; Sep. 8am–6pm; Oct. 9am–5pm ● DM4; groups DM3/pers.; children free* 🔲 🔲 🔲

The small white castle on peacock island was built to look like a Gothic castle in ruins, complete with oak paneling, towers and an iron bridge. The idea for this design came from Wilhelmine von Encke, the mistress of Frederick-Wilhelm II. After 1797, the castle was turned into a holiday home for the family of his grandson, Frederick-Wilhelm III. Inside is a curious collection of Biedermeier-style hats that once belonged to Queen Luise.

### Kavalierhaus (2)
#### In the park on Pfaueninsel

Ⓒ *May–Aug. 8am–8pm; Sep. 8am–6pm; Oct. 9am–5pm ● interior closed to the public*

The 'house of the Cavalier' is the most impressive building on the island. The elaborate façade, the work of the important Berlin architect Friedrich Schinkel, was inspired by a house in Danzig in which a great-uncle of Arthur Schopenhauer used to live. Unfortunately, its large salons are not open to the public.

### Rinderstall (3)
#### In the park on Pfaueninsel

Ⓒ *May–Aug. 8am–8pm; Sep. 8am–6pm; Oct. 9am–5pm ● closed to the public*

The Rinderstall (stable) dates from 1802. The graceful Gothic style is reminiscent of the medieval farm buildings of the Brandenburg countryside. Horses and calves still graze in the fields on the island.

### Gedächtnistempel für Königin Luise (4)
#### In the park on Pfaueninsel

Ⓒ *May–Aug. 8am–8pm; Sep. 8am–6pm; Oct. 9am–5pm ● closed to the public*

Standing on the edges of a small wood, this temple was built in memory of the late Queen Luise by Karl Friedrich Schinkel. The marble bust captures the beauty of this much-loved queen of Prussia.

## Not forgetting

■ **Wirtshaus zur Pfaueninsel** Pfaueninselchaussee, Berlin (Zehlendorfd) ☎ (030) 8052225 Ⓒ Oct.–Apr.: Wed.–Mon. 9am–8pm; May–Sep.: daily 9am–11pm *A rustic restaurant serving traditional Berlin food. In summer you can enjoy a drink on the terrace.*
■ **Blockhaus Nikolskoe** Nikolskoer Weg, Berlin (Zehlendorf) ☎ (030) 8052914 Ⓒ Fri.–Wed.: 16 Apr.–Oct. 10am–10pm; Nov.–15 Apr. 10am–8pm *Traditional German food and wonderful views over the Wannsee area.*

The park, transformed into an English-style garden in 1822, is today a nature reserve.

*Havel*

PFAUENINSEL

BERLINER FORST

N

On peacock island, neo-Gothic follies contrast with sober classical buildings.

107

## Basic facts

The Schloßpark Glienicke, the grounds of the palace built during the reign of Frederick-Wilhelm II, forms a natural border between Berlin and Potsdam. In 1824, Prince Charles, the son of Queen Luise, made it his summer residence and then, until 1989, it became part of the Royal Palace

# Further afield

### Schloßpark Kleinglienicke (5)
**Königstraße 36, Berlin (Zehlendorf) ☎ (030) 8053041**

Ⓜ *Wannsee* 🕐 *daily* ● *free* 🍽 ♿ 🅿

The grounds of the Schloß were planted from 1816 by the landscape artist Peter Joseph Lenné. At the request of Prince Charles, he created an English garden, adorned with neoclassical pergolas and temples.

### Schloß Glienicke (6)
**In the grounds of Kleinglienicke ☎ (030) 8053041**

🕐 *15 May–15 Oct.: Sat., Sun., public holidays 10am–5pm* ● *DM3; concessions DM2* 🍽 *DM4*

In 1825, Prince Charles engaged the architect Karl Friedrich Schinkel to transform his modest manor house into a splendid classical palace. Inside, you can see the large room overlooking the grounds, the majestic staircase and the Weiße Zimmer (White room) which is still furnished with period furniture.

### Große Neugierde (7)
**In the grounds of Kleinglienicke**

🕐 *daily* ● *free* 🍽 ♿

The two rotundas guarding the entrance to the Glienicker Bridge are known as Große and Kleine Neugierde (large and small curiosity). They were built by Schinkel (1835–37) as lookout posts to oversee the traffic on the main avenue between Berlin and Potsdam.

### Klosterhof (8)
**In the grounds of Kleinglienicke**

🕐 *on request* ● *DM4* 🍽 *guided tours only*

The Klosterhof (1850) is a copy of an early Christian-Byzantine monastery on the Venetian island of Chartreuse. On the east wall, the sarcophagus of the philosopher Pietro d'Abano comes from St. Anthony's in Padua.

### Glienicker Brücke (9)
**Königstraße 36, Berlin (Zehlendorf)**

Ⓜ *Wannsee* ♿ 🅿

Between April 1945 and November 1989, this bridge was the scene of many meetings between Americans and Soviets. Famous for being the place where spies were swapped on misty mornings, it has since played a leading role in many spy films. The views are breathtaking, with Schloß Babelsberg to the south and the Heilandskirche to the north.

## Not forgetting

■ **Remise Glienicke** Königstraße 36, 14163 Berlin (Zehlendorf) ☎ (030) 8054000/8059901 🕐 Tue.–Sun. 7pm–9pm ➡ 54.

of Sanssouci ➥ 110. The gardens.

**Havel**

**VOLKSPARK KLEINGLIENICKE**

Berliner Str.

Königstraße

Mövenstraße

**SCHLOẞ BABELSBERG**

N

5

6

One of Berlin's beautiful parks stretches along the banks of the Havel.

5

6

7

9

8

## Basic facts

The glorious Sanssouci Park is the setting for palaces, castles and baroque follies. Modeled on Versailles, it took around a century to complete, from the reign of Frederick the Great to that of Frederick-Wilhelm IV. Covering more than 700 acres, the park is a marvelous

 # Further afield

## Schloß Sanssouci (10)
### In the grounds of Sanssouci, Am Grünen Gitter, 14414 Potsdam
### ☎ (0331) 9694200, 9694202

Ⓜ *Potsdam Stadt, then the 695 bus* 🕒 *Grounds daily Palace Apr.–Sep. 9am–5pm; Oct.–Jan. 9am–3pm; Feb.–Mar. 9am–4pm; closed Mon. ● DM10; concessions DM5* 🈲 *DM15; concessions DM8* 🈲 🈴 

Built in 1744 by Frederick II, the magnificent rococo palace of Sanssouci soon became his favorite residence. The most interesting room is the library with its cedar paneling and bronze and gilt decoration.

## Neues Palais (11)
### In the grounds of Sanssouci, Hauptallee

🕒 *Apr.–Oct., Feb.–Mar. 9am–5pm; Nov.–Jan. 9am–3pm; closed 12.45–1.15pm and Mar. ● DM10; concessions DM5* 🈲 *DM15; concessions DM8* 🈲 🈴 🅿

The New Palace is another of Frederick the Great's projects. With more than 400 rooms, it is the largest of the palaces in Sanssouci Park.

## Bildergalerie (12)
### In the grounds of Sanssouci, An der Maulbeerallee

🕒 *15 May–Oct. 10am–5pm; closed Mon. ● DM4; concessions DM2* 🈲 🅿

Frederick II used this Prussian rococo picture gallery to exhibit his collection of paintings by Italian, French and Dutch masters.

10

11

evocation of the style of the 18th century.

**Potsdam/Sanssouci**

## Chinesisches Teehaus (13)

🕐 15 May–15 Oct. 10am–5pm; closed Fri. ● DM2

Frederick the Great used this teahouse to store his collection of oriental porcelain; it bears witness to the 18th-century passion for China. Statues, recently regilded, representing musical scenes and Chinese figures drinking tea, stand around the building.

## Orangerie (14)

🕐 15 May–15 Oct. 10am–5pm; closed noon–1pm and Thur. ● DM5; concessions DM3 🍴 ☕ 🅿

At the northern end of the grounds, this palace was built in 1848. Its façade, modeled on those of Medici and Pamphili residences, reflects the Kaiser's passion for Italy. The Raphael hall, not to be missed, contains more than 50 copies of masterpieces by the Italian artist and other Renaissance painters. In winter, the hothouse in the left wing shelters palm trees and exotic plants that spend summer out on the terraces.

## Not forgetting

■ **Café im Drachenhaus** Maulbeerallee, in the grounds of Sanssouci ☎ (0331) 291594 🕐 Apr.–Oct. 11am–7pm; Nov.–Mar. 11am–6pm *Coffee, cakes and a small selection of hot dishes.*

## Basic facts
The ancient Brandenburg town of Potsdam was once the favored
residence of intellectuals, none more famous than the French
philosopher, Voltaire. The city is a mixture of red and yellow: the yellow
façades of the baroque town houses lining the pedestrian area and the

 # Further afield

### Holländisches Viertel (15)
#### Mittelstraße et Benkertstraße

Following a trip to the United Provinces (now the Netherlands) in 1732,
Frederick-Wilhelm I decided to construct a Dutch village in the center
of Potsdam. He called upon the help of Johan Baumann, who built 134
red-brick houses between 1733 and 1744. These were intended as
homes for the court craftsmen from Holland; it was hoped they would
encourage other Dutch people to move to the city. However, the
project was a failure and the houses were eventually inhabited by
soldiers and Prussian workmen. The buildings at the crossroads of
Mittelstraße and Benkert Straße were among the first examples in the
Old World of the Dutch influence in architecture that was to become so
popular during the second half of the 18th century. The area was
miraculously spared during World War II and is today a lively area of
cafés, art galleries, and expensive stores.

### Nauener Tor (16)
#### Friedrich-Ebert-Straße/Hegelallee

In 1755, Frederick the Great had his architect build the Nauen Gate.
Inspired by engravings of the Scottish castle of Inverary, the Kaiser wanted
to imitate its neo-Gothic style – hence the battlements and two pointed
towers. The Gate marks the northern entrance to the old town.

### Peter-Pauls-Kirche (17)
#### Bassinplatz ☎ (0331) 2804942

🕙 Sat. 5–6pm (mass: Mon., Wed., Thur. 8am; Sun. 7.30am, 10am, 7pm) 🅿

Dedicated to the saints Peter and Paul, this church is the largest
Catholic sanctuary in Potsdam. Its apse was modeled by the architect
Schinkel on the one at St. Sophia's in Istanbul; the bell tower is an exact
copy of the one at San Zeno's in Verona. Of particular note inside are
the three paintings on the side altars, works of the painter Antoine
Pesne who was a favorite artist of Frederick II.

### Brandenburger Tor (18)
#### Luisenplatz

Like Berlin, Potsdam has its own Brandenburg Gate. Erected in 1770 by
Frederick the Great to commemorate the Prussian victory during the
Seven Years' War, this Roman triumphal arch is slightly older than its
more famous Berlin counterpart, if somewhat smaller. The avenue
running alongside the pedestrian area joins the Peter-Pauls-Kirche to the
town gates and is lined with beautiful ocher buildings.

## Not forgetting
■ **Juliette** Jägerstraße 39 ☎ (0331) 2701791 🕙 daily Mon.–Sat.
11.30am–11pm (reservation recommended) *French food in an elegant setting.*
■ **Luise** Luisenplatz 6 ☎ (0331) 903663 🕙 Mon.–Sat. 8am–11pm; Sun.
8am–6pm *Italian dishes and regional German cooking. Friendly service at the bar.*

red brick of the charming houses in the Dutch quarter.

Stalin, Truman and Chuchill attended the Potsdam Conference (1945) to work out the details of future peace treaties in Europe.

15

15

17

15

18

16

18

## Basic facts

Neuruppin is today known as 'the gateway to Ruppin', a hilly area full of woods and lakes, just 45 minutes to the northeast of Berlin by car. This small town on the banks of Lake Ruppin is a favorite haunt of Berliners taking a break from city life.

# Further afield

### Klosterkirche (19)
**An der Uferpromenade ☎ (03391) 397260, 2597**

🕙 *Apr.–Oct. 10am–4pm* ● *DM1; DM2 including entrance to the tower* 🈵 💱 🎫 🅿

The Klosterkirche, built of red brick in 1246 as a Dominican convent church, is one of the few buildings to survive the fire of 1787 which destroyed most of the town of Neuruppin. The church, now Protestant, is becoming a venue for concerts.

### Schinkeldenkmal (20)
**Kirchplatz**

Neuruppin is the birthplace of Karl Friedrich Schinkel (born 1781; died Berlin 1841), painter, architect, and the grand master of Prussian neoclassicism. A statue has been erected in honor of the town's famous son at no. 8 Fischbänkerstraße, not far from the Predigeerwitwenhaus (the house of the preacher's widow), his childhood home.

### Fontanedenkmal (21)
**Karl-Marx-Straße**

The people of Neuruppin have also erected a statue to another of its famous sons, the novelist Theodor Fontane (1819–98). The writer is shown as a resting pilgrim, wearing a hat and carrying a stick. His parents used to own the Löwen Apotheke (the Lion's Pharmacy) on the same street. It was with great affection that Fontane dedicated one of his works to his home town, *Wanderungen durch die Mark Brandeburg* (*Walks through the Brandenburg Countryside*).

### Tempelgarten (22)
**Präsidentenstraße**

🕙 *May–Oct. 10am–6pm* 🈵 *Tourist information office ☎ (03391) 2345* 🍴 🅿

This peaceful refuge was built by Georg Wecceslas von Knobelsdorff (the architect of the palace of Sanssouci ➡ 110), at the request of Frederick II while he was still heir to the throne and commander of the Neuruppiner Regiment. The baroque style of the palace contrasts sharply with the surprising eastern architecture of the Moorish Türkische Villa. The latter now houses a charming café-restaurant.

## Not forgetting

■ **Altes Kasino** Seeufer 11/12 ☎ (03391) 3059 🕙 daily 7–10.30am *Good home cooking and regional dishes.*
■ **Café im Tempelgarten** Türkische Villa, Tempelgarten, Präsidentenstraße 89 ☎ (03391) 2122
🕙 11am–midnight; closed Mon. *Snacks, coffee and cakes. Young clientele.*
■ **Salonschiff mit Gastronomie** Seeufer ☎ (0171) 8205664
*In summer, enjoy a meal on the waters of Lake Ruppin, in winter, a meal anchored off the Uferpromenade.*

Neruppin inspired the descriptions of 19th-century Brandenburg found in Effi Briest, by Theodor Fontane.

## Basic facts

Berlin and the surrounding countryside (notably around Brandenburg) is the ideal location for people wishing to go horseback or play tennis or golf. If you like swimming, there is the mile-long beach along the shores of the Wannsee.

# Further afield

### Horse racing: Galopprennbahn Hoppegarten (23)
**Goetheallee 1, 15366 Dahlwitz/Hoppegarten**
**☎ (03342) 38930**

◷ *Tours 8am–4pm* **Racing season** ☎ *(03342) 389323* ◷ *Apr.–Oct.* ● *DM7 standing (concessions DM3.50); DM20 terraces; DM40 stands* 🔲 🏢 🍴 🔲 🅿

Thoroughbreds have raced on this course since 1868. From spring until the fall, it hosts prestigious international races, culminating, on October 3 (the anniversary of German reunification), with the Zino Davidoff Grand Prix.

### Golf: Sporting Club Berlin Scharmützelsee e.V. (24)
**Parkallee 3, 15526 Bad Saarow ☎ 033631/630**

◷ *daily approx. 8am–10pm* ● **Practice range** *DM20; concessions DM10; DM5 for 40 balls* **Green Fees** *DM80; concessions DM40; Sat., Sun. DM100; concessions DM50* 🔲 🍴 🔲 🔲 🅿 🔲 *at the weekend*

Built in 1955, this golf club, along with its vast sports center, is one of the largest in Europe. Three 18-hole courses, designed with the help Bernhard Langher, Nick Faldo, and Arnold Palmer, cover over 750 acres on the picturesque banks of the Scharmützelsee. You must prove that you are a member of a golf club in your home country to be allowed to play these prestigious courses.

### Tennis: Tennis-Turnier-Club 'Rot-Weiß' (25)
**Gottfried-von-Cramm-Weg 47–55, 14193 Berlin (Wilmersdorf)**
**☎ 030/89575520 ➠ 89575551**

🅜 *Grunewald* **Courts** ◷ *daily 6 Oct.–12 Apr.* ● *indoor courts DM34/hour* **Tournaments** ● *DM25–150/day* 🍴 🔲

Situated in the elegant district of Grunewald, this tennis club is the home of the German Open, which takes place around mid-May, attracting the world's top players to what is the most important women's tournament in Germany. Indoor and outdoor courts are available for rent throughout the year.

## Not forgetting

■ **Horseback riding: Landshaus Bott** Friedrich-Engels-Damm 300, 15526 Bad Saarow ☎ (033631) 63350 ◷ Mon.–Thur. 10am–11pm; Fri.–Sun. 8am–11pm *At an elegant country hotel.*

■ **Golf: Seehotel Waldfrieden** Am See 27, 15864 Wendisch Rietz ☎ (033679) 6090 ◷ daily 7am–10pm *Play at a charming country house then enjoy regional cooking on the terrace.*

■ **Tennis: Grand Slam** Gottfried-von-Cramm-Weg 47-55, 14193 Berlin (Wilmersdorf) ☎ (030) 8253810 ◷ Evenings; closed Sun.–Mon. ➥ 54 *Haute cuisine prepared by the chef, Johannes King, and awarded a Michelin star.*

23

23

24

24

25

25

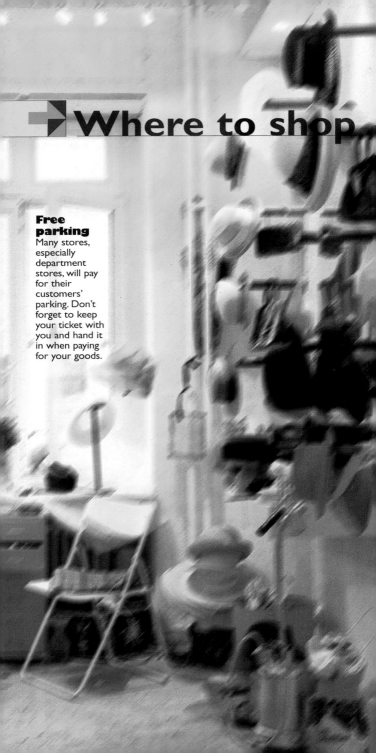

# Where to shop

## Free parking

Many stores, especially department stores, will pay for their customers' parking. Don't forget to keep your ticket with you and hand it in when paying for your goods.

## Opening hours

Most stores open Monday to Friday from 9.30am to 6.30pm, and Saturday from 9am to 2pm. Late-night shopping is usually on Thursday until 8pm. On the first Saturday of every month, most stores stay open until 6pm.

# 33
# Shops

THE INSIDER'S FAVORITES

## Taxes

If you spend more than DM60, you can claim the tax back (between 6 and 11%) from customs when you leave the country. Make sure fill out the correct form in the store. You will have to produce your passport for identification.

## In the area
Any shopping spree should start at the Wittenbergplatz. When the sun shines, take time out to relax on one of the benches around the square and enjoy the entertainment provided by the city's buskers.
■ Where to stay ➡ 26 ■ Where to eat ➡ 38 ■ After dark ➡ 66

# Where to shop

## Kaufhaus des Westens (1)
### Tauentzienstraße 21–24, Berlin (Schöneberg) ☎ (030) 21210

🅜 *Wittenbergplatz* **Department store** 🕐 *Mon.–Fri. 9.30am–8pm; Sat. 9am–4pm* ▭

This famous department store, which opened in 1907, it is Europe's largest department store. Beloved by Berliners and Germans alike, it is hardly ever called by anything but its nickname: 'KaDeWe'. It was spruced up in 1996, and its seven floors of merchandise look even more appealing as a result. You are guaranteed to find what you are looking for: from a simple button to haute couture, from a slice of bread to fresh caviar, each department has an outstanding range of goods. A few examples:

**Second floor** A vast perfume and cosmetics department. You will also find hundreds of pairs of pantyhose and socks in every shape, color, and style imaginable, as well as all the major lines of skin care products and make-up.

**Third floor** The Mode-Straße (Fashion Street) provides the setting for every style-conscious woman's dream. All the major fashion houses are represented here, including Escada, Armani, Bogner, and Zapa, to name but a few.

**Fifth floor** The legendary china department, with its amazing selection from 56 different makes, including Meissen, Royal Copenhagen, Wedgwood, Hermès, and KPM. The glassware department offers the largest selection available anywhere in Germany, stocking 36 different manufacturers, including the French Baccarat et Sèvres and the Swedish Kosta Boda and Orrefors.

**Seventh floor** This is the most tantalizing floor of all, a paradise for food connoisseurs and food lovers alike, a veritable temple to gastronomy. A "seventh heaven" indeed. The shelves are filled with products and ingredients that tantalize the senses with flavors and smells from the four corners of the world: teas from India, mushrooms from Morocco, oysters from Brittany, and chicken from Bresse. In all, the shelves display around 1700 different types of cheese, more than 1000 kinds of sausage and ham, 800 different breads and a selection of wines to satisfy even the most demanding palate. During the hunting season, the department stocks whole wild boars, mouth-watering cuts of venison and all types of game bird. Fresh fish is available all year long. Naturally, the KaDeWe prides itself on stocking only the freshest produce available. And for those for whom the sights and smells of such a cornucopia of culinary delight are not enough, scattered around the department you will find counters where you can taste these delicacies. Is it any wonder that Berliners often make their way here for a little something to eat?

## Not forgetting

■ **Schuhtick (2)** Tauentzienstraße 5, Berlin (Charlottenburg) ☎ (030) 2140980 *Reasonably priced shoes and other footwear, in all styles, shapes and colors.*
■ **Lichthaus Mösch (3)** Tauentzienstraße 7a, Berlin (Schöneberg) ☎ (030) 2148630 *Stylish lamps and fashionable lighting, with products from Germany, Italy, and Spain.*

■ What to see ➠ 94

Before reunification,
KaDeWe was a potent
symbol of West Berlin's
consumer society.

## In the area

The stores along the Kurfürstendamm divide into two quite distinct styles: upmarket stores toward the Adenauerplatz; colorful boutiques at the other end. ■ Where to stay ➡ 24 ■ Where to eat ➡ 36 ➡ 40 ■ After dark ➡ 66 ➡ 68 ■ What to see ➡ 94

 # Where to shop

## Boutique Granny's Step (4)
**Kurfürstendamm 56, Berlin (Charlottenburg) ☎ (030) 3237660**

Ⓜ *Adenauerplatz* **Women's clothes and accessories** 🕒 *Mon.–Fri. 10am–6pm; Thur.; 10am–8pm; Sat. 11am–1pm* ▭

The designer Ruth Demmer offers exclusive outfits, elegant cocktail dresses, and evening gowns. Only the best fabrics are used – pure silk, lace and velvet. The boutique also stocks a selection of hand-made hats, purses and gloves to complete the look.

## Budapester Schuhe (5)
**Kurfürstendamm 199, Berlin (Charlottenburg) ☎ (030) 8811707**

Ⓜ *Uhlandstraße* **Men's shoes** 🕒 *Mon.–Wed. 10am–6pm; Thur.–Fri. 10am–8pm; Sat. 10am–4pm* ▭

This shoe store specializes in classical styles from Hungry, Austria, the United States, Italy, and England, with an emphasis on smart oxfords. Whether they are made by Alden, Tod's, Budapester Schuhe, or Moreschi, all are hand-sewn. Some designs are made of rare leathers, such as crocodile skin, but priced at an astonishing DM3000 to DM4000 a pair, they find few takers.

## Gallerie Pels-Leusden (6)
**Fasanenstraße 25, Berlin (Charlottenburg) ☎ (030) 8826811 (Villa Grisebach)**

Ⓜ *Uhlandstraße* **Drawings and prints** 🕒 *Mon.–Fri. 10am–6.30pm; Sat. 10am–2pm*

Established in 1950, this art gallery is one of the most famous in Berlin. Even if you're not around for one of the auctions organized by the gallery in the fall and spring, you'll still be tempted by some of the paintings (large and small), lithographs or drawings by contemporary artists that are exhibited here throughout the year.

## Erich Hamann – Bittere Schokoladen (7)
**Brandenburgische Straße 17, Berlin (Wilmersdorf) ☎ (030) 8732085**

Ⓜ *Konstanzer Straße* **Chocolate** 🕒 *Mon.–Fri. 9am–6pm; Sat. 9am–1pm*

Credit for the simple beauty of this store is due to the wife of the owner, Anna Hamann, who had it refurbished in the Bauhaus style in 1927. All their chocolates are home-made. Pure paradise for chocaholics, particularly fans of dark chocolate (up to 70% cocoa).

## Not forgetting

■ **Das provençalische Fenster (8)** Bleibtreustraße 19, Berlin (Charlottenburg) ☎ (030) 8815518 *Scarves, shoes, and sweaters for women.*
■ **Anselm Dreher (9)** Pfalzburger Straße 80, Berlin (Wilmersdorf) ☎ (030) 8835249 *Art gallery selling modern art from around the world.*

The statue (opposite) stands at the entrance to the Gallerie Pels-Leusden, attracting passers-by to view prints and drawings.

## In the area

With its fashionable cafés and famous restaurants, the area around the verdant Savignyplatz attracts those looking to relax, away from the hubbub of Berlin. This calm, residential area is home to many small boutiques in which it is pleasant to browse and shop.

# Where to shop

### Friederike Fiebelkorn (10)
**Bleibtreustraße 4, Berlin (Charlottenburg)** ☎ **(030) 3123373**

Ⓜ *Savignyplatz* **Women's clothes** Ⓢ *Mon.–Fri. 11am–7pm; Sat. 11am–4pm*

This boutique specializes in the work of Berlin designers, including creations of the proprietor herself. Whether you're looking for day or evening wear, classic styles or something more striking, all the clothing is beautifully cut, made from top quality fabrics. Dresses are made to measure, and although the prices are high, those in the know judge that they are still good value, especially when compared to prices in the boutiques of Paris and Rome.

### Arno (11)
**Savignyplatz, Berlin (Charlottenburg)** ☎ **(030) 3129010**

Ⓜ *Savignyplatz (under the railroad arches)* **Lamps, furniture** Ⓢ *Mon.–Fri. 10am–8pm; Sat. 10am–4pm* ▬

Arno is truly an Aladdin's cave of stylish lamps. Classic designs by the likes of Kreon, Matrix, and Luceplan hang from the vaulted ceiling, illuminating a selection of designer couches, chairs, and tables by ES and Triangolo.

### Der Küchenladen (12)
**Knesebeckstraße 26, Berlin (Charlottenburg)** ☎ **(030) 8813908**

Ⓜ *Savignyplatz* **Silverware, cooking utensils** Ⓢ *Mon.–Fri. 10am–7pm; Sat. 10am–4pm* ▬

This small, friendly store is just the place if you're looking for a particular kitchen implement, or if you're stuck for ideas on what to buy that friend who already has everything. No matter how many times you visit, a trawl around this fascinating store always turns up something new — and if you are really at a loss for an idea, perhaps you can offer that friend something as exclusive as a tiny truffle grater!

### Seidlein & Seidlein (13)
**Bleibtreustraße 49, Berlin (Charlottenburg)** ☎ **(030) 3124480**

Ⓜ *Savignyplatz* **Interior design** Ⓢ *Mon.–Fri. 11am–8pm; Sat. 10am–4pm*

The Seidleins stock fabrics, china, and furniture made of the finest materials. The emphasis is on French and English country style, but there are also designs from the Brixton Pottery in Britain and ceramics by Hedwig Bollhagen of Brandenburg.

## Not forgetting

■ **Kaufhaus Schrill (14)** Bleibtreustraße 46, Berlin (Charlottenburg) ☎ (030) 8824048 *Eccentric and interesting fashions and accessories for men and women.*
■ **Secondo (15)** Mommsenstraße 61, Berlin (Charlottenburg) ☎ (030) 8812291 *Good quality second-hand clothes including many designer labels. Some real bargains for both men and women.*

Where to eat
➡ 34
After dark ➡ 72

Kantstraße

Grolmanstr.

Carmerstr.

Savigny-platz

Schlüterstraße

M *Savignyplatz*

Bleibtreustraße

Niebuhrstraße

Knesebeckstraße

Grolmanstraße

Mommsenstraße

N

10

13

3

11

39

12

14

15

KÜCHENLADEN

## In the area

You'll discover a great area for shopping to the south of the Ernst-Reuter-Platz, one of Berlin's major crossroads. Many stores line Knesebeckstraße, Schlüterstraße and Grolmanstraße, and there are plenty of enticing café terraces when you need a break!

 # Where to shop

### Kiepert (16)
**Hardenbergstraße 4–5, Berlin (Charlottenburg) ☎ (030) 311880**

Ⓜ *Ernst-Reuter-Platz* **Bookstore** Ⓢ *Mon.–Fri. 9am–8pm; Sat. 9am–4pm* ▭

The largest bookstore in Berlin, with years of experience catering for a public said to be the most intellectually demanding in Germany. With more than four floors, the store has books on every subject including a large paperback section and a well-stocked department on antiques and collectibles. On a more practical level, you can also find books and videos about Berlin and the Brandenburg countryside.

### Confiserie Mélanie (17)
**Goethestraße 4, Berlin (Charlottenburg) ☎ (030) 3138330**

Ⓜ *Savignyplatz* **Confectionery** Ⓢ *Mon.–Fri. 10am–7pm; Sat. 10am–1pm* ▭

In this magical candystore, Eberhard Päller sells around 4000 types of candy and other sweet (and some savory) delicacies from around the world. Several products are made according to secret family recipes handed down through the generations, and many others are still handmade by small confectioners throughout Germany. The shop offers a tempting array of treats: rows of filled pralines are displayed near spices and relishes from the far corners of the world, and French butter candies next to top-quality German mustard.

### La Gioia (18)
**Knesebeckstraße 17, Berlin (Charlottenburg) ☎ (030) 3136598**

Ⓜ *Savignyplatz* **Women's clothing** Ⓢ *Mon.–Fri. 11am–6.30pm; Sat. 11am–4pm* ▭

Meike Bergner stocks a personal and sophisticated selection of scarves, wraps, and hosiery. Everything from evening gowns, skirts, sweaters, coats, and jewelry to the smallest handkerchief reflects the owner's preference for simple and elegant cuts and colors.

### Berliner Zinnfiguren (19)
**Knesebeckstraße 88, Berlin (Charlottenburg) ☎ (030) 3130802**

Ⓜ *Savignyplatz* **Model soldiers** Ⓢ *Mon.–Fri. 10am–6pm; Sat. 10am–3pm* ▭

Werner Scholtz's store is the only one of its kind in Berlin. Thousands of brightly-colored toy soldiers rest waiting to re-create the great battles of history, from the Prussian crusades to the Native American charges. This is a place of pilgrimage for collectors of toy soldiers, and those with a more strategic bent will also find a section devoted to military literature. The selection of toy soldiers from the reign of Frederick II and the Napoleonic Wars is unrivaled.

## Not forgetting

■ **Rosewaters Bath & Body Shop (20)** Knesebeckstraße 5, Berlin (Charlottenburg) ☎ (030) 3134242 *The place to go for top-quality bath and body products. Stock imported from France and Great Britain.*

■ Where to eat ➡ 34
■ After dark ➡ 64 ➡ 66

Ernst-Reuter-Platz

Bismarckstraße

M Ernst-Reuter-Platz

Schillerstraße

Hardenbergstraße

Goethestraße

Schlüterstraße

Knesebeckstraße

Grolmanstr.

N

Mélanie's SPEZIALITÄTEN

17

A wonderful selection of sweets and specialties from around the world at Mélanie's.

17

18

18

19

19

# In the area
This famous avenue, along with the nearby Friedrichstraße, has undergone some radical changes since reunification. The upmarket stores that have opened here have returned the area to its former glory.
■ Where to stay ➡ 18 ➡ 28 ■ Where to eat ➡ 48 ■ After dark

# Where to shop

## Meißener Porzellan (21)
**Unter den Linden 39b, Berlin (Mitte) ☎ (030) 2043581**

Ⓜ *Unter den Linden* **China** Ⓢ *Mon.–Fri. 10am–7pm; Sat. 10am–4pm*
Ⓗ *Kurfürstendamm 213, Charlottenburg* ☎ *(030) 88683530* ▭

All the pieces in this store are marked with crossed blue swords, the mark of the prestigious workshop of Meissen, near Dresden. It was here that the technique for making hard-paste porcelain was first discovered. A large selection of dinner services, figurines, and other ornaments are available, both new editions and original patterns.

## Galeries Lafayette (22)
**Französische Straße 23, Berlin (Mitte) ☎ (030) 209480**

Ⓜ *Französische Straße (in the Frierichstadt-Passagen, area 207)* **Deparment store** Ⓢ *Mon.–Fri. 9.30am–8pm; Sat. 9am–4pm* Ⓟ *underground* ▭

This Paris institution recently opened a branch in Berlin. Its reasonably priced clothes present a vision of French style, and the food hall, in the basement, offers a selection of French delicacies. The Gallic influence is equally present in the perfume, jewelry, and leatherware departments.

## Bürgel-Haus (23)
**Friedrichstraße 166, Berlin (Mitte) ☎ (030) 2044519**

Ⓜ *Französische Straße* **Pottery** Ⓢ *Mon.–Sat. 9am–8pm* ▭

This store specializes in dark-blue pottery with white stippling, made today, as it was in the Middle Ages, in the small city of Bürgel en Thuringe. It also stocks a large selection of blue fabrics.

## Frankonia (24)
**Friedrichstraße 69, Berlin (Mitte) ☎ (030) 8857390**

Ⓜ *Stadtmitte (in the Friedrichstadt-Passagen, area 205)* **Ready-to-wear** Ⓢ *Mon.–Fri. 10am–8pm; Sat. 9am–4pm* ▭

One of the largest stores in Germany specializing in hunting outfits and regional costumes (*Trachten*). The store also sells traditional clothing for both men and women by Meindl and Gössl, leather clothes and accessories by Joop, Boss, and Bogner, and smart casual wear by Barbour and Timberland.

# Not forgetting

■ **Berlin-Kosmetik (25)** Friedrichstraße 167, Berlin (Mitte) ☎ (030) 2012220/2012221 *Cosmetics form Berlin-based companies Koivo and Indra, and salespeople who offer good advice.*
■ **Der Teeladen (26)** Friedrichstraße 67 (in the Friedrichstadt-Passagen, area 205), Berlin (Mitte) ☎ (030) 20945892 *Two hundred different types of tea from around the world.*
■ **Escada (27)** Friedrichstraße 176, Mitte ☎ (030) 2386443 *The largest Berlin branch of this ready-to-wear label, stocking elegant, classic, and brightly-colored designs. Also on sale: shoes, accessories, and perfumes.*

➡ 60
■ What to
see ➡ 78
➡ 80

GALERIES LAFAYETTE

Where else would the
French department
store Galeries
Lafayette be than in
Französische Straße
(French Street)?

## Basic facts

Almost every neighborhood in Berlin has its own flea market. Unfortunately, most antique and second-hand dealers only have stalls at the weekend, but there are a few places where you stand a good chance of discovering hidden treasure even during the week, too. If that's your

# ➡ Where to shop

### Kunst- und Trödelmarkt (28)
**Straße des 17. Juni, Berlin (Charlottenburg) ☎ (030) 26550096**

Ⓜ *Ernst-Reuter-Platz, Tiergarten* **Crafts, second-hand goods** 🕙 *Sat.—Sun. 10am—5pm*

This is the largest and most famous of Berlin's flea markets. To the left, crafts. To the right, second-hand goods: particularly furniture, East German army memorabilia, records, and books.

### Berlin Antik-und Flohmarkt (29)
**Under the S-Bahn viaduct 190—203**
**Georgenstraße/Friedrichstraße, Berlin (Mitte) ☎ (030) 2082645**

Ⓜ *Friedrichstraße* **Antiques, rare objects** 🕙 *Wed.—Mon. 11am—6pm* ▬

Sixty small stores have joined together to make up this slightly pretentious antiques market under the S-Bahn viaduct. One shop specializes in teddy bears and valuable old games, and in others there is 18th, 19th and 20th-century furniture, clothing from the 1920s, antique jewelry, pottery, coins, medals, and old books.

### Berliner Kunst- und Nostalgiemarkt (30)
**Kupfergraben et Am Zeughaus, Berlin (Mitte)**

Ⓜ *Unter den Linden* **Crafts, second-hand goods** 🕙 *Sat.—Sun. 11am—5pm*

This is a popular spot with tourists, given the proximity of the market to Museuminsel (Museum Island) and the saxophone

28

28

aim, get an early start to avoid the crowds that gather as the day goes on.

players who add to the lively atmosphere. This market is famous for its crafts and is the ideal place to find gifts. Don't bother with the bits of stone that are said to be from the Berlin Wall!

## Bücherstand vor der Humboldt-Universität (31)
### Unter den Linden, Berlin (Mitte)

Ⓜ *Unter den Linden* **Books** 🕐 *daily 10am–5pm*

Because it is next door to the university, the stalls of this market are always varied and well-stocked, particularly with low-priced second-hand novels. Some of the booksellers specialize in sought-after rare editions of art books from the former GDR.

### Not forgetting

■ **Winterfeldmarkt (32)** Winterfeldplatz, Berlin (Schöneberg)
🕐 Wed., Sat. 8am–1pm *One of the most colorful of Berlin's markets and a favorite meeting place for Berliners. Second-hand stalls and many cafés.*
■ **Fehrberliner Platz (33)** Brandenburgische Straße/Hohenzollerndamm, Berlin (Wilmersdorf) 🕐 Sat.–Sun. 8am–4pm *One of the most typical of Berlin's markets. Everything from large furniture to tiny gadgets. Rather kitsch but fun.*

# Finding your way

**X9** Flughafen Tegel Airport

**109** Airport Tegel über Ku'damm

**N21** Märk. Viertel Wilhelmsruher D.

**N48** S-Bhf Nikol

**Watch the PLZ !**

What we know today as Berlin was once a group of independent towns and villages. For this reason, many districts (*Bezirke*) have streets of the same name. Make sure you know which district or postal code (PLZ, *Postleitzahl*) a street belongs to!

S+U-Bahnhof Zoolog. Garten

# 12 Maps

## Street vocabulary

**Allee**: alley
**Bezirk**: district, area
**Brücke**: bridge
**Chaussee**: (main) road
**Damm**: sidewalk (or embankment)
**Garten**: garden
**Graben**: ditch (road built by a ditch)
**Park**: park
**Platz**: square
**Schloßpark**: grounds of a castle or palace
**Straße**: road
**Tor**: gate
**Ufer**: bank, shore

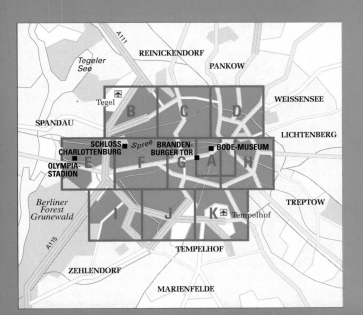

# Street index

For each street, the letter in bold refers to one of the maps (A–K), and the letters and numbers mark the square in which it is found.

# Index

# Transport map

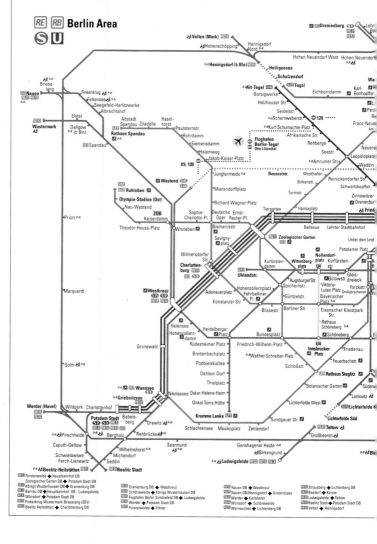

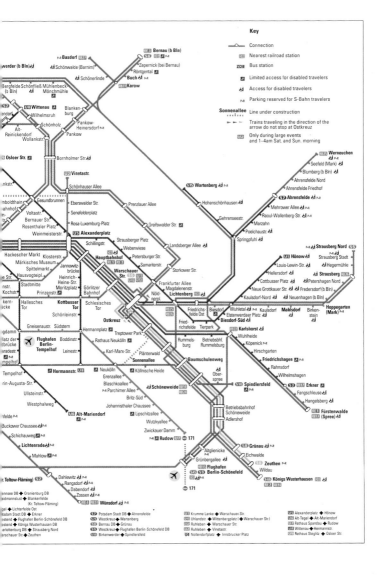

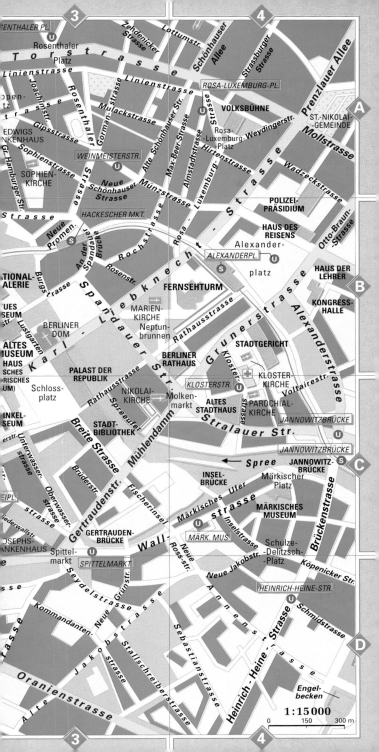

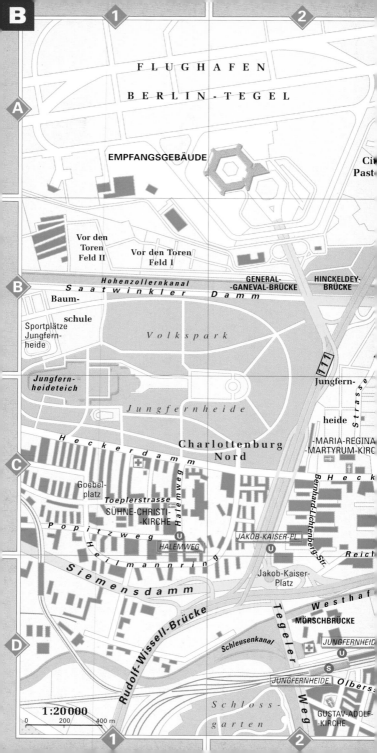

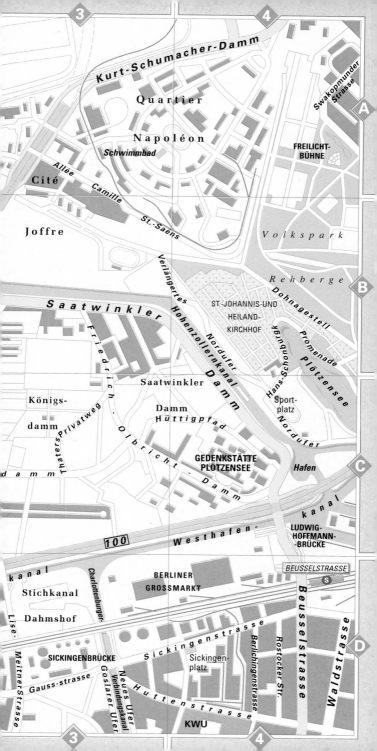

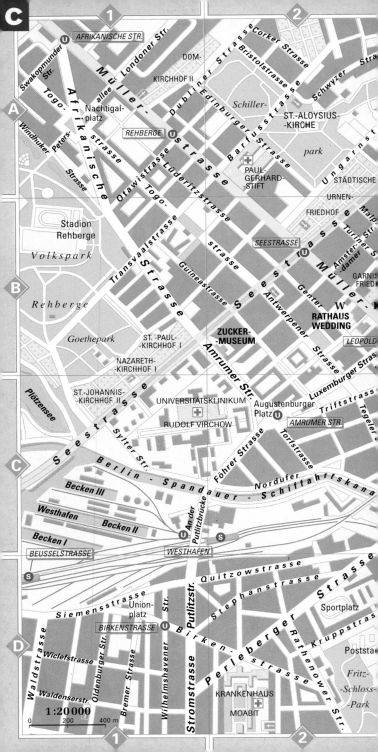

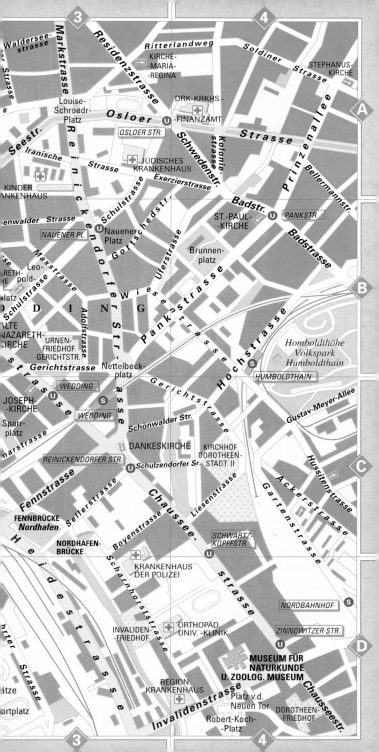

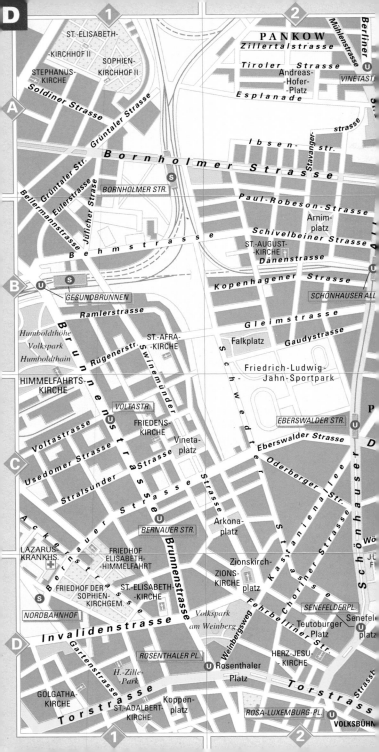

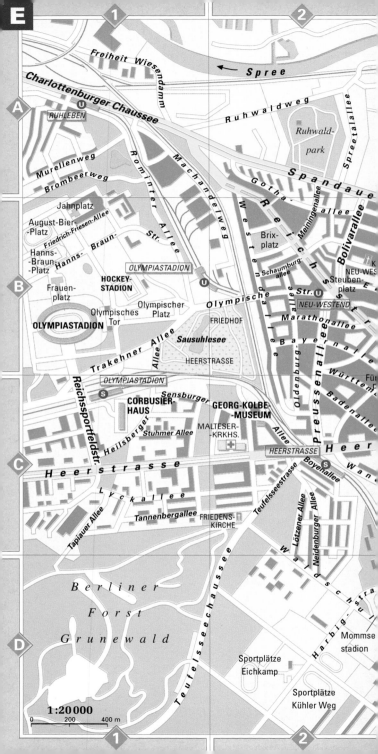

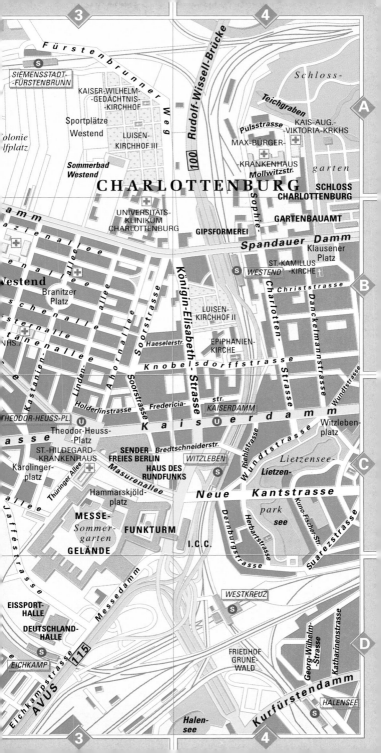

**F**

**1** **2**

GUSTAV-ADOLF-
KIRCHE

Brahestrasse

Gauss-str.

Schwarzer

Weg

Hut

Lise-Meitner-Str.

Neues Goslarer

Charlottenburger

Osnabrücker Strasse

Mierendorffplatz

**A**

*Schloss -*

*Karpfen-
teich*

MARIÄ-
HIMMELF.-
KIRCHE

**U** MIERENDORFFPL.

Sömmeringstr.

Nordhauser Strasse

Goslarer
Platz

*garten*

Mierendorffstr.

Quedlinburger Str.

**U** CAPRIVIBRÜCKE

Ufer Verbindungskanal

Ufer

Tegeler Weg

**SCHLOSS
CHARLOTTENBURG**

SCHLOSSBRÜCKE

Charlottenburger Ufer

Am Spreebord

Spree

RÖNTGENBRÜCKE

DO
BRÜ

GARTENBAUAMT

Luisen-
platz

Eosanderstrasse

**Damm**

ÄGYPTISCHES
MUSEUM

Wintersteinstr.

Otto

HERZ-JESU-
KIRCHE

LIETZOW-
KIRCHE

*Spandauer*

**ANTIKEN-
MUSEUM**

BRÖHAN-
MUSEUM

Gierkepl.

R.-Wagner-
Platz

**RATHAUS
CHARLOTTENBURG**

Guer

Klau-
sener
Platz

ST.-KAMILLUS-
KIRCHE

**B**

Schustehrus-
str.

Kaiser-

str.

**U**

Suhr- Allee

LUISEN-
KIRCHHOF I

Nehringstrasse

Schloss-strasse

LUISENKIRCHE

RICH.-WAGNER-PL.

Cauer

Seelingstrasse

Hebbelstr.

Haubachstr.

Richard-Wagner-Str.

Friedrich-

Wilmersdorfer

Danckelmannstrasse

Knobelsdorffstr.

Fritsche-

Zillestrasse

**DEUTSCHE
OPER BERLIN**

**LANDES-
ZENTRALBAN**

Wundtstr.

Spielhagen-
str.

DEUTSCHE OPER

**U**

Sophie-
Charlotte-
Platz

**B i s m a r c k s t r a s s e**

**SCHILLER
THEATER**

**U**

**Kaiserdamm**

FINANZAMT
CHARLOTTENBURG

BISMARCKSTR.

ST.-
THOMAS-KIRCHE

**BUNDES-GER.
KAMMER-GER.**

SOPHIE-
CHARLOTTE-PL.

Schillerstr.

Karl-
August-
Platz

*Witzleben-
platz*

Windscheidstrasse

**S c h i l l e r s t r.**

**C**

*Lietzen-
see*

Witzlebenstr.

Pestalozzistrasse

**G o e t h e s t r.**

Leibnizstrasse

Wielandstr.

Schlüterst.

Suarezstrasse

ST.-CANISIUS-
KIRCHE

**K a n t s t r a s s e**

TRINITATISKIRCHE

**K a n t**

Amtsgerichts-
platz

WILMERSDORFER STR. **U**

Friedbergstr.

Stuttgarter
Platz **S**

SAVIGNYPL.

Rönnestrasse

CHARLOTTENBURG

Lewishamstr.

N i e b u h r s t r.

Niebuhrstr.

M o m m s e n s t r.

Giesebrechtstr.

Holtzendorff-
platz

Gervinus-

Sybel-

strasse

Wilmersdorfer Str.

Sybelstrasse

Leibnizstrasse

Wielandstr.

Schlüterstrasse

**D**

Heilbronner Str.

Karlsruher Str.

Joachim-Friedrich-Str.

Droysenstr.

Damaschkestr.

Dahlmannstr.

Adenauer-
platz

**U** ADENAUERPLATZ

Brandenburgische Strasse

Olivaer
Platz

Konstanzer Str.

Bayerische Str.

Paris

**K u r f ü r s t e n d a m m**

**SCHAUBÜHNE**

**K u r f ü r s**

Westfälische
Strasse

Nestorstr.

Paulsborner Strasse

Duisburger
Str.

Düs

ST.-ALBERTUS-
MAGNUS-
KIRCHE

1:20000

0   200   400 m

Hoch-
meister-
platz

NEUAPOST.
KIRCHE

KONSTANZER STR. **U**

**1** **2**

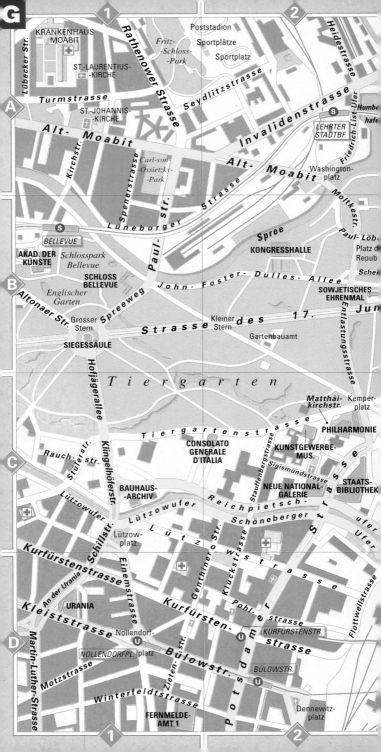

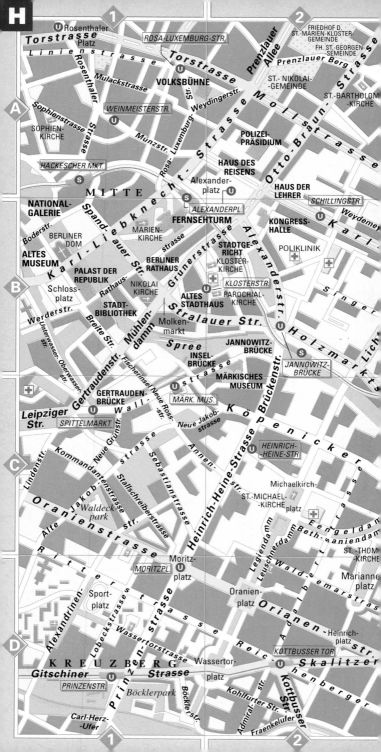

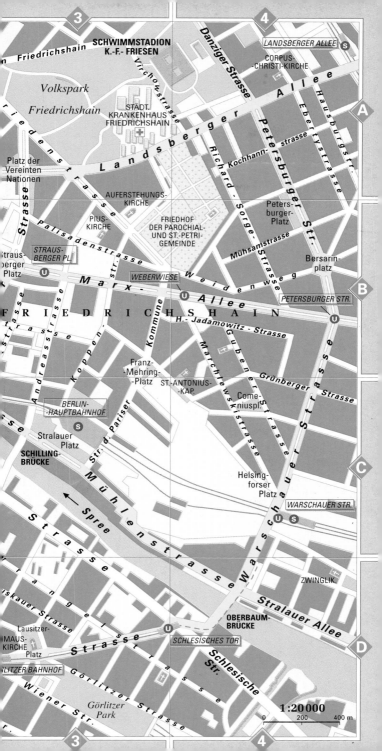

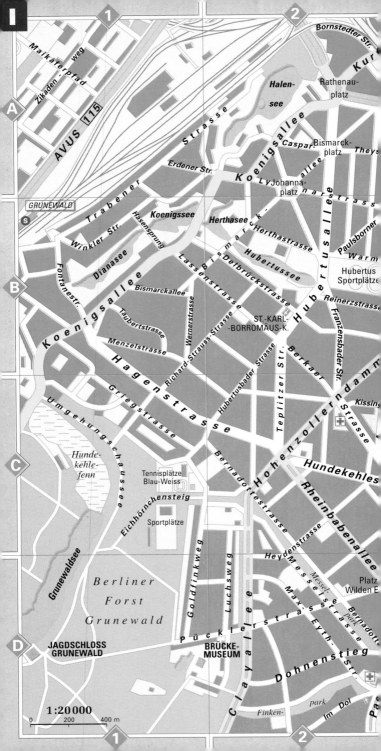

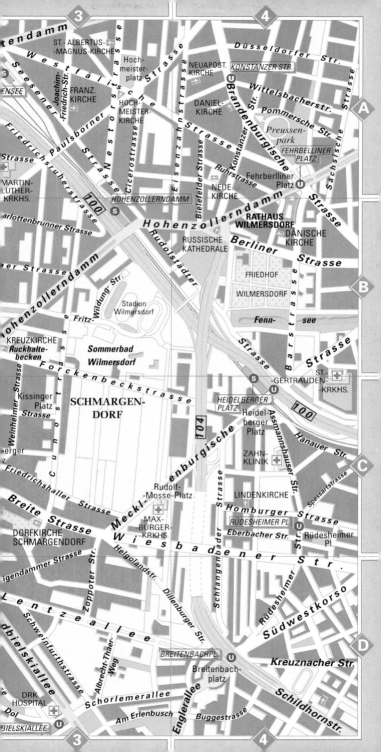

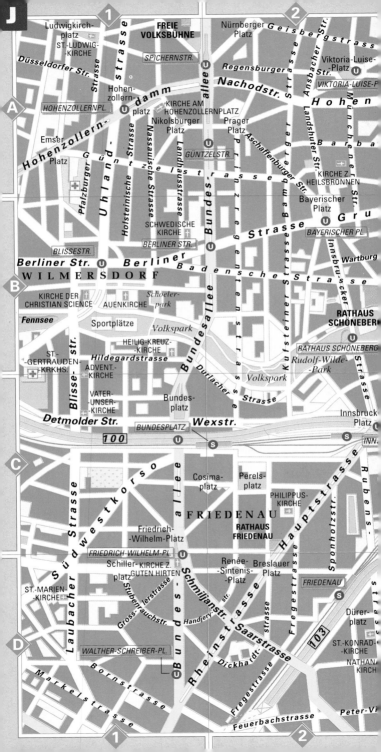

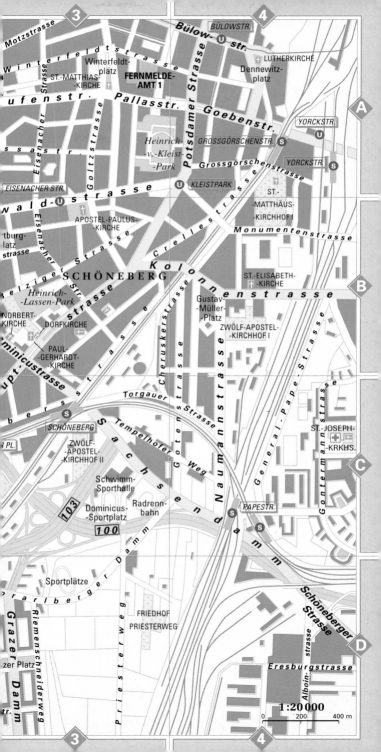

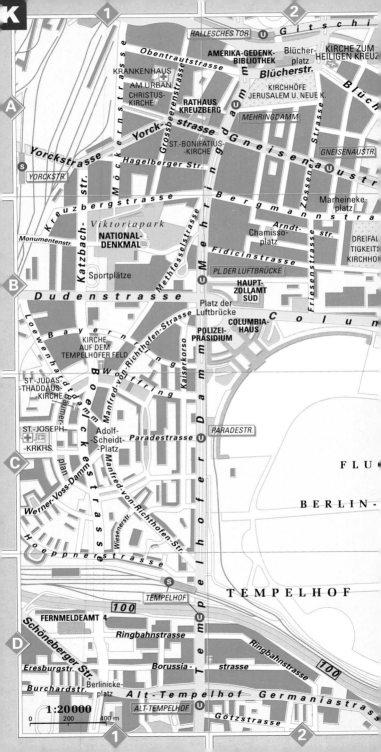

The listings in this guide are presented in alphabetical order in this general index. Each section in the book opens with an index based on another form of classification. For an overview of the guide, see the table of contents ➡ 3.

We would like to thank the Berliner Verkewhrsbetriebe Gesellshaft and the Deutsche Bundesbahn for their cooperation.

## Picture
# Credits